UNHERALDED

BRENT MELLOY

*To Audrey, who loved Texas high school
football almost as much as I do*

*To Robert Belew for being a great mentor
and showing me the way in this world*

To my wife Joy, my best friend and the love of my life

CONTENTS

PREFACE

On December 22, 1990, the Vernon Lions met the Crockett Bulldogs for the Class 3A Texas state championship in football. The prior year Vernon had lost the title game to Mexia by a score of 21-20. Future hall of fame coach Leo Brittain had coached a lot of really good teams on his way to the 1990 finals. Playing for "state" the prior year had only served to motivate the Vernon Lions to finish the job. Having graduated from Vernon High and having played football for coach Brittain gave me a certain perspective on this particular game.

In 1979 when I was a senior in high school, Vernon was no different from any other town in Texas. As was the norm, the fall semester of school revolved around football. It all began in the weeks preceding the start of school each year when all of the boys, freshman through senior, gathered for "two-a-day" practices. The start of 1990 was different in that the expectations for quarterback Ken Collums and running back Derrick Richardson were extremely high. Coach Brittain was on the verge of garnering his first state championship.

Although Brittain had already established a respectable winning record, the one thing he coveted was a state championship on his resume. Having coached in the Texas high school ranks for some time, Brittain knew that winning a state title in football put one in rarified air. Many successful football coaches never win a championship. The win over Crockett in 1990 placed Leo Brittain among the elite and ultimately led to his induction into the Texas High School Coaches Association Hall of Fame in 2009. There are so many things I remember growing up as a young man in rural Vernon, Texas. The things I remember most, though, are the things from being a part of the high school football team, and more specifically, the things I learned from being around a winning personality such as coach Brittain.

I developed a passion for Texas high school football at an early age. I blame my addiction on Dave Campbell's *Texas Football* magazine. Known as the "Bible" of all things football in Texas, it became the one thing I looked forward to most each summer. I devoured every issue, cover to cover. I'm still not certain why I became so enamored with all of those statistics, but I did.

In 1990 I arrived in the Richmond-Rosenberg area, about thirty-five miles southwest of Houston, Texas. My initial impression of the area was that it had that small town feel. People were very friendly, and the twin cities had a laid-back atmosphere. The towns were close enough to Houston to be a convenient drive, but far enough that the big city did not encroach on peoples' lives. As the Vernon Lions were wrapping up their state title, I wondered about the status of football in Richmond-Rosenberg. I knew that Lamar Consolidated High School had a decent reputation in the Houston area, but no titles to their name. It was 2005 before I really started paying attention to the local sports scene. It was around that time that I started hearing the neighborhood kids talk about these two brothers who were bringing a lot of excitement to the Mustang football program. Then the winning started and I realized Lamar was a legit program capable of making a big splash in the Texas UIL football playoffs. I started going to the games and I was quickly introduced to the talent of the Rodgers brothers. James, the oldest, and his younger brother by one year, Jacquizz, were making statements every week on the football field. It did not take long to get caught up in the excitement that permeated Lamar Consolidated High School.

The players were reading a local newspaper one day and started noticing that there was little to no coverage of the Mustangs. I contacted the editor of the paper and offered to submit game reports which entailed getting to know the coaching staff and the players. They all appreciated my endeavors, and I got a chance to become involved in what was happening. What was most fascinating about the whole thing was learning how driven these young men were in a single-minded pursuit of their common dream. They had a plan, and they knew what it would take to be successful. They were disciplined and they had an incredibly high degree of accountability both amongst themselves and from their coaching staff. I felt compelled to share their story, which is a textbook on sacrifice, accountability, teamwork, and winning.

Brent N. Melloy DVM
April 2021

2007 LAMAR CONSOLIDATED MUSTANGS

TEAM ROSTER

2 Mark Faison	26 Errol Nolan	70 Jerell Spears
3 DD Goodson	27 Gary Scott	71 Eric Thompson
4 Corey Hodge	31 Julius Smith	72 Paul Alford
6 Quentin Palmer	32 Anthony Duckett	73 Jarret Cobbin
7 Andrew Okokhere	33 Jacquizz Rodgers	74 Deante Ester
8 Brandon Camp	36 Justin Goodson	75 Jose Pena
9 Marcel Threat	37 Jeremy Simmons	76 Antoine Everett
10 Teddy Robinson	40 Jonathon Taylor	78 Coris Owens
11 Steven Fleming	41 Ashton Laday	80 Calvin Kimble
12 Carlos Becerra	43 Sule Osagiede	81 Travis Riedel
14 Kyle Greer	50 Taylor Turner	82 Tremell Nicholson
15 Darrell Smallwood	51 Josh Gonzales	83 Adan Gomez
18 Chuck Obi	52 Colin Usen	84 Cory Green
19 Jarrod Seahorn	56 Presley Godson	85 Dominique Briggs
20 Jamal Williams	60 Alex Rohde	86 D'Vonn Brown
21 Nick Gardner	62 Beny Bravo	87 Andrew Nwaogwugwu
22 Mason Quintanilla	65 Robert Brown	89 Charles Taylor
23 Jeff Okonye	66 Josh Kaluza	
24 Skylar Patterson	67 Clarence Ward	

2007 LAMAR CONSOLIDATED COACHING STAFF

HC Lydell Wilson
OC Pat Matthews
DC Lane Wade

Staff

Charlie Ayro	Jimmy Franklin	Greg Kobza
Jason Callahan	Roy Hernandez	Steve Hummel
Ronnie Humphrey	Pat Peloquin	Luis Romero
Gerald Thompson	Jeff Urinak	John Velasquez
Dennis Fyke	Lance Hale	

SECTION I

CHAPTER 1

THAT PERFECT SEASON... NOT

Alamo Heights

The yellow school bus rolled into the parking lot of the Round Rock Independent School District stadium. **Lamar Consolidated** was emblazoned across the side in black letters above the three black regulation stripes. Then a second bus rolled in behind and Coach Lydell Wilson was already on the steps, eagerly awaiting the opening of the doors. The team's stay at the downtown hotel had not been as restful as he had hoped, and the waiting around all day had Wilson with second thoughts about bringing his team to Round Rock the day before the game. To this point in their perfect season, they had driven to the games the day of. For the semi-final contest against San Antonio Alamo Heights, Wilson thought it might be a good change of pace to arrive the day before.

Linebacker Sule (Soo-lay) Osagiede (Oh-saw-gu-day) was the first one off the players' bus and was flashing his patented smile. Behind him were sophomore quarterback Darrell Smallwood Jr. and junior running back Jacquizz Rodgers. As the three Mustangs huddled outside the bus door, they were joined by senior defensive back James Rodgers, Jacquizz's older brother. As they chatted, the smile on Osagiede's face suddenly turned into his other familiar look... the game-time scowl. His change of attitude came from spying one of the opposing players across the Round Rock playing surface. Enemy sighting.

The Division 1 Class 4A semi-final game between the San Antonio Alamo Heights Mules and Houston area Lamar Consolidated figured to be the same for the Mustangs in that they would play great defense and try to get Jacquizz Rodgers going early. They came into Round Rock riding on an impressive and school record thirteen game winning streak. The Mustangs knew going into the 2006 season that they were going to be formidable. Boasting no less than four certain division one (D1) college recruits in the senior class and probably several more who were underclassmen, the Mustangs easily overmatched their opponents in class 4A and even the 5A opponents they had faced.

Defensive lineman Levar Brown was recruited by the University of Arizona and was a pure beast. Offensive lineman Jarvis Jones had signed with LSU but would eventually transfer and start for the Oklahoma Sooners. And then there was Mr. Highlight Reel himself, James Rodgers. On any given Friday night James (Quon to his teammates) could be seen returning a kickoff for a touchdown, catching a touchdown pass, or collecting a pick six. And it wouldn't be surprising to see him do all three in the same game.

Under center for Lamar was sophomore quarterback Smallwood, DJ to his troops. Possessing a muscular frame, DJ could have been a linebacker or fullback, except he had a cannon for an arm and was deadly accurate with the long ball. As warm-ups came to a close, the Mustangs became antsy to get the show started. This would be the night they would punch their ticket to the school's first ever trip to the state championship. The chatter on the sidelines and in the stands rose to a frenzied level.

With Brown and Deante Ester lined up on the ends, the defensive line was stout. Behind them were inside linebackers Osagiede and senior Jarrod Coss. The outside linebackers were Ed Obregon and Garland Harris Jr. James Rodgers headed up a shut down secondary. However, the older Rodgers brother was dealing with a severe ankle sprain suffered in a 40-10 quarterfinal win over Caney Creek. James and Sule were in on a tackle together and had collided. Rodgers hobbled off knowing it wasn't good. For Alamo Heights he took some Advil and had the ankle heavily taped.

Mustang athletic trainer Lance Hale saw how badly the ankle affected Rodgers. "His sprain was severe. We taped it as best we could, but it was obvious that he was affected by it. He basically could run in a straight line. There was no way he could make the cuts that made him such a dynamic player. He wasn't the same."

Osagiede was also nursing an injury. His right knee had begun to swell more with each game from about the midpoint of the season. As he entered the training room all he could think was … two more games. Osagiede could only rub the tender knee as he watched the trainer skillfully tape his ankles. The junior linebacker wanted so badly to be the leader today, Lamar's first ever time in the semis. But he would take a backseat to Quon, Levar, and Jarvis. He would let those seniors lead them to the championship game and then next year would be his turn to be the man.

Shaheed Davis held down one cornerback spot and junior Carlos Becerra the other. Not a lot was known about Alamo Heights outside of what was seen in the film of their Area win over New Braunfels. Thus far the Mustang defense had not had any trouble handling opposing offenses. Few teams could run effectively on them, and this made them almost impossible to pass on. Which only served to make their own vaunted rushing attack on offense, led by sensational junior running back Jacquizz Rodgers, all the more lethal. Once the grinding Mustang offense hung a few scores on an opponent, the game was pretty much over. Quizz was already setting records at Lamar in just his second season as a full-time starter. There was no reason in their minds that tonight would be any different for the Mustangs.

Across the field, standing in their way, was a surging Alamo Heights squad that had rattled off thirteen straight wins of their own after a season opening loss to Class 5A Georgetown. Quarterback Giovanni Vizza's star was on the rise having mastered Coach Don Byrd's spread offense. After transferring from Central Catholic, Vizza had used his junior year learning and perfecting the new offense. Lamar head coach Wilson knew that containing Vizza, who was also an excellent runner, was the key to the game for his defense. Likewise, Mule's coach Byrd knew his defense needed to contain Jacquizz Rodgers.

Coach Byrd felt he had a good team after they got past New Braunfels 31-21 in the Area round. "We were not picked to beat either New Braunfels or Lamar Consolidated. Getting past New Braunfels was a boost to our confidence. We started off the season with a loss to Georgetown, which I attributed to our still trying to work things out in all three phases: offense, defense and special teams."

Once Alamo Heights got things locked in, they became increasingly competitive as the season progressed, especially on the defensive side of the ball. Coach Byrd felt the Mules' defense never really got the credit they deserved for the team's immense success that season mainly because Vizza and Dibrell and those guys on offense had put up big numbers. "We would get out ahead of folks and then the defense would just create havoc. We had a good run into the playoffs the year before and then ran into a really good La Marque team. Still, as coaches, we had that taste in our mouths and our kids absolutely despised losing."

This was Lamar's first time in Kelly Reeves Athletic Complex. The stadium was built around 2003, and the paint still looked fresh. As I entered the stadium the two teams were warming up on the Astroplay artificial surface. The virtually untested Mustangs were strutting through warm-ups, brimming with confidence. The Lamar swagger was on full display. None of the teams they had faced had figured out how to slow down the vaunted Mustang rushing attack. And their defense was always bigger and faster than opposing offenses. As warmups came to a close, Wilson looked at Quon and the other team leaders and felt they were clearly the more talented bunch. They exuded a confidence that had taken several years to achieve. Now, tonight, the machine was humming on all cylinders. The town had turned out in full force as they had also gotten accustomed to winning after so much losing prior to Wilson's return to Lamar. As kickoff time neared, the Mustangs emerged from the locker room adorned in their navy-blue jerseys and silver pants and were designated the home team. The Mules would be the visitors and wore their traveling white jersey with gold pants uniforms.

After sizing up the Mustangs, Coach Byrd knew he would need to use his spread offense effectively to offset the fact that his offensive line was not as big as the guys they were blocking. "Gio ran the spread offense really well, and Sam Dibrell's height and athleticism gave him an advantage." The Mules either had a one back or no back set and tried to get Vizza out in space with the run-pass option, just getting the ball to the receivers in the flats. The game started well for Heights, but Lamar was changing up their secondary to keep Byrd guessing and that is what led to the interception that almost changed the momentum in the second half.

The Mules raced out to a 21-0 halftime lead. Although the Mustang offense had driven into Heights territory four times in the first half, they were not able to capitalize, with two of those series ending with interceptions. This was something Smallwood had managed to avoid for most of his sophomore season. Lamar also had a punt blocked late in the second quarter that led to a last-minute touchdown when Vizza found Dibrell for another score. The spread offense was working its magic. Ester, Lamar's big defensive end, knew the Mustangs came in probably a little too confident. "We were loaded on the D-line with myself, Dillon Quintanilla, Levar Brown, and Andrew Nwaogwugwu (Wah-goo-goo). The problem was that Heights made zero mistakes in that first half. We expected to run over everybody and that didn't happen."

Lineman Jarvis Jones recognized the problem for the Lamar offense. "Alamo Heights overloaded the box multiple times to stop our running game and it also affected our ability to throw the deep ball." The Mules defense would bend but not break. Then, on offense, Heights relentlessly attacked the second level with quick passes to the flats, often lining up four receivers. The Heights offense threw running back Colton Haverda at defenses until he was stopped, and then Vizza made them pay with the read option.

Byrd had his team in the right frame of mind. He made sure they knew of the doubters in the media. Vizza remembers the week leading up to the semi-final contest: "We knew they were a very good team with tons of talent that included a handful of D-1 guys. We knew about the Rodgers brothers mainly. The talk in the press was about how we were overmatched athletically. The underdog role fit us well. We made a point to hit 'em in the mouth early. The media said it would be a blowout. They were right."

Lamar came out in the second half and drove for a touchdown, with Quizz scoring on a four-yard run. Then Mustang receiver Flint Gardner, filling in on defense, collected his second interception of Vizza and ran it back to the Mules three-yard line. Quizz took it in from there to cut the lead to 21-14. At that point, the Lamar sideline came alive, and it looked like the Mustangs had finally settled in. In the stands, I could feel a collective sigh of relief amongst the Mustang faithful on the North side of the stadium. Coach Byrd knew his offense needed to do something big. And he knew exactly what to do: get the ball in Gio's hands out in space and let him determine the outcome of this game. Lamar linebacker Cory Green saw the misery the Mustangs felt in the game because of one specific play. "They kept running the same basic quarterback rollout run-pass read option over and over and our secondary could not stop it."

"Things got a little tense after that second interception and quick score," said Byrd. "Rodgers began to do his thing. Anytime you have a big time back on a team coming out of the Houston area you have to know they are going to do some damage. It was huge that our offense came back and scored on the next drive." Vizza found Dibrell again for another touchdown and Alamo Heights quickly regained the momentum. Heights scored two more times and the game ended 42-14. A stunned Lamar crowd witnessed their Mighty Mustangs lose for the first time that season. But it was how they lost that was so shocking. As the final seconds ticked, I found myself still glued to my seat, trying to process the game that just was.

The noise from the clanging of rubber soles on the metal bleachers finally died down. The stunned Lamar Consolidated faithful were heading for the exits. Some were still there, unable to move, not quite sure what to think. Their faces had gone blank in disbelief. The Mustangs had come in as favorites and only once gotten close. Quizz was standing at the edge of the field with one hand on the chain link fence, the other tugging on the neck of his number 33 jersey. His mind was racing, and his face showed the disappointment.

What just happened here? This wasn't the plan.

The game that just ended kept replaying in his head. He glanced one more time at the scoreboard, but the numbers would not change.

ALAMO HEIGHTS	**42**
LAMAR CONSOLIDATED	**14**

What just happened here?

Friends and family had come to the fence to console him. He heard their words, but his lack of expression showed he really was not hearing anything. His older brother James had quickly exited into the locker room with the other Mustangs. Coach Wilson would be huddling them up, making sure they knew how proud he was of them and how special this season had been. But the young man who remained outside just could not let go of the fence. It would mean admitting defeat.

This wasn't the plan.

He kept glancing into the now mostly empty stands, his eyes darting left and right. The look of hurt on his face made one's stomach clench. Quizz reluctantly let go of the fence, hugged his family, and departed the Round Rock ISD field.

Mustang linebacker Garland Harris felt they had let this one slip away too easily. "Heights passing game was better than any we had faced. They had obviously studied us better. Maybe if Flint had been inserted sooner on defense. But who knows?" Vizza attacked Lamar's shorter corners with his taller receivers. Gardner had the height to match up with Dibrell, but the Mustang coaches had no way of knowing that he would perform so well on defense.

Many in the Lamar stands were fearful that the Mustangs had just blown their best chance ever to go to state. Graduation would take a heavy toll. The Mules went on to defeat Robert Griffin III and the Copperas Cove Bulldawgs in the Alamodome the following week, winning 40-28, going away, for the school's first and only state championship. When Vizza reflected, he knew they had to play perfect to do what they did to some good teams. "Lamar had so much talent, you know. They really were a good team. Their quarterback was a sophomore, and that's a lot to ask of somebody that young."

Coach Wilson echoed these sentiments. "It was the first time all year that DJ had played like a sophomore. But there was plenty of blame to go around." Alamo Heights clearly had the better game plan on this night.

The bus ride back to Rosenberg was somber. Ester remembers the disgust. He knew they had not just lost but had gotten their butts kicked. They had never experienced that. "We were disappointed then, but in hindsight, it may have been what us underclassmen needed. We carried that chip on our shoulders all of the next year."

Defensive back Quentin Palmer remembers feeling bad for the seniors who would not get another chance. "Biggest thing that stood out to me was the hurt to our marquee players. Levar Brown literally bit his cast off. The seniors from that year were cut deep. All they had heard was how we were the team to beat that year." If only they could turn the clock back to the opening kickoff. Maybe they could have had a little more of a sense of urgency. If only.

Coach Mike Zierlein knew they had been beaten by a hot team at the time. He was personally proud of how the guys battled back from being down 21-0 so quickly. "We got within a TD and then Heights completed a huge pass just over the fingertips of Shaheed Davis that could have just as easily been a pick six the other way. After that it basically crumbled on us. Coach Byrd and his staff had a good plan. On paper Lamar maybe had more talent but got outplayed and outcoached. That happens if one is in this game long enough."

Lamar cornerback Shaheed Davis echoed these sentiments. "We came in overconfident and underestimated a team that was hot at the time. We prepared physically but not mentally. We got ahead of ourselves." With the way

Heights flawlessly executed, there was not any room for the mistakes Lamar made, which were mostly mental. Alamo Heights defeated them soundly and it was humbling.

A golden opportunity had slipped right through their fingertips. Who knew when they would get another chance at state? The next year would be one of rebuilding depleted offensive and defensive lines. Quizz tried not to think about the game that just was, and how his and James' plan would never come to fruition. He would have plenty of time to think about the future later. The brothers still had basketball and track seasons together. On the bus he closed his eyes and hoped to wake up anywhere but Round Rock, Texas.

The Rodgers brothers' uncle Rodney Williams was in the stands that evening and felt disappointment on several levels. "They had too much talent to go down like that. We really felt they had blown their best chance." On top of that the family was still trying to get James signed to play college ball. Texas State was in the picture, but this was before Oregon State. Rodney felt a good performance in a state championship game would have helped James' cause. Now that was gone. In the end it all worked out though.

James hung around Richmond until June before heading off to Corvallis, Oregon on a football scholarship. He and Quizz worked out daily at the Lamar field house. After James left, Quizz needed to come up with a new plan. It started with relentlessly throwing himself into his workouts. The field house was the one place he could sort it all out. It was time to move forward and leave the devastating loss at Round Rock in the past. Several on the team had their eyes opened and were stunned. A team that was loaded with D-1 talent, one many thought was headed to state, had gone home empty handed. The lesson was not lost on anyone, certainly not Quizz or Sule.

CHAPTER 2

A TRAIN RUNS THROUGH

Mr. Rodgers' Neighborhood

The twin towns of Richmond-Rosenberg are located about thirty-five miles southwest of the Houston metroplex. Richmond lies to the east, and Rosenberg to the west, although the towns are inseparably joined at the hip by US Highway 90-A. Driving into downtown Richmond, one crosses the Brazos River bridge into town center. Richmond is the county seat of Fort Bend County. When I first arrived in 1990, the population of Richmond was around 12,000 with Rosenberg only slightly larger. The area had a small town feel to it even though it was relatively close to Houston. The US Census Bureau reported that the area was approximately 55% Hispanic, 20% white Caucasian, and 17% African American.

Driving in for the first time, I immediately recognized that Richmond was typical of all of the other small Texas towns I had ever driven through. The buildings were small, single story types, and cars lined the streets in angled parking spots making it difficult for two-way traffic but something I was accustomed to. In front of the small county courthouse stood a statue of Mirabeau Buonaparte Lamar, the second president of the Republic of Texas. He had been buried near Richmond in 1859 and was considered instrumental in the early development of the region. There are many streets and a handful of schools named in his honor throughout the state of Texas much like his predecessor, Sam Houston, who was the first president of the Republic. After driving through the small downtown, I realized I could have just as easily been back in my childhood hometown of Vernon. On the right was a popular hangout called Jaime's Dairy Treat, although the sign was faded and difficult to read at first glance. I had to stop and check out the little burger joint, wondering how it had managed to survive against the McDonalds and Burger Kings of the world.

Highway 90-A becomes Jackson Street in the town of Richmond. It changes again into Avenue H after passing FM 3155, which is also known as Collins Street. It is all part of the confusing way Texas tends to give streets multiple names. At the intersection of Collins and Jackson, I came across the large Southern Cotton Oil mill run by Archer Daniels Midland Corporation. The old mill was built alongside the railroad tracks, making the hauling of product convenient for the Union Pacific trains that rolled through Richmond-Rosenberg. Crossing over the tracks revealed a part of town that consisted of small houses crammed together on short streets. Some of the cars parked under carports had not been driven in quite some time as evidenced by missing tires and weeds growing up through the radiator grills. I wondered about the purpose of the bathtub sitting in one yard. The constant humming of window air conditioning units filled the air as they faced a constant battle against the never-ending Gulf Coast heat and humidity. The whole scene was a far cry from the master planned subdivisions along Highway 59 to the south of town. The local convenience store clerk informed me that this area was referred to as the "Heights."

Collins Street dead ended at George Park, which backed up to the Brazos River. On the left at the intersection of Collins and George Avenue was Thomas Lane Pink Elementary School where many of the 2007 Mustangs began public schooling. Across the street from this was the old Richmond City Park that at one time was full of children playing football and other sports. Now the bleachers were all rusted out and the boards were cracked and rotting. The small field was overgrown with weeds. As I walked across the field, I could almost hear the kids yelling and screaming. I could see the parents in the now-dilapidated stands on a Saturday afternoon, cheering their youngsters on to victory while trying to find shade beneath the two pecan trees. Several neighborhood homes backed up to the little city park. If one were lucky enough to know the homeowners, the games could be viewed from shaded back patios. As I neared the backstop, I could see the place in the dirt where home plate once resided. Suddenly, the old park seemed to whisper to me: "Where have all of the children gone? We had so much fun." But it was just the wind blowing the tops of the dandelions far, far away. The little park was now barely a reminder at best.

Tasha Williams was born and raised in Richmond and grew up in the small part of town north of the train tracks. James Rodgers was a local boy as well and lived near Tasha in high school. They developed a romance and soon had two sons. James Jr. was born on December 20, 1988. Jacquizz followed on February 6, 1990. The brothers were inseparable from the start. Tasha remembers the boys being typical brothers. "They couldn't stand being outdone by the other. It was a constant competition, and it didn't matter that Quizz was younger, he never used that as an excuse."

Tasha ended up raising the boys by herself as James Sr. was in frequent trouble with the law. "I knew I was pretty much on my own. Their father couldn't stay out of trouble. I decided my sons were not going down that path." Tasha used a firm hand with her boys, and fortunately they were good kids. She always said she trusted them and allowed them to choose their friends. Kids are generally more perceptive than the adults around them realize. James and Quizz tended to avoid kids who were criticized by their mother. She raised her sons to be humble and amenable. Tasha was a track athlete in middle school. She qualified for the Jesse Owens finals in California after winning her age group in the Texas regionals. She finished second nationally. The single mom obviously passed down her athleticism to her sons.

While the boys generally could sleep thru the glaring of the train horn, Tasha often found herself marking the wee hours of nighttime by it. As the rumble of the trains passing through town pierced through the silence, she often lay awake wondering how she would navigate through an uncertain world with two small boys who were depending on her to mold them into young men. Thankfully, she had family nearby to help. But the responsibility of raising her children fell squarely on her young shoulders. It seemed to her that just yesterday it was she that was the carefree teenager with no responsibilities outside of just her own. That all had seemed to change overnight. And the train's horn was there to remind her that life, much like the train itself, kept rolling on, never stopping for anything or anyone.

Rodney Williams was a large part of his sister Tasha's support structure. He remembers his sister being the fastest kid in sixth grade, boy or girl. She loved to run track and play other sports. Then she had to grow up fast once she had children of her own. "She was a young mother, but she did a helluva job raising those boys the right way. She taught them to be disciplined and respectful." Tasha deferred to her brothers, Michael and Rodney, for sports related activities, but she was the one who got credit for the men that James, Quizz, and their younger siblings, Michael and Cartai, became.

Living in this part of town meant either playing football or baseball at the City Park or riding down to George Park on their bicycles. Those that didn't have bikes could still make the walk. George Park had actual baseball fields and other sports venues. If there was money available, the kids could walk up Collins to the small convenience store for candy and sodas. Sometimes they would walk all the way up Collins to the tracks and place pennies on the rails just before the train went by. The flattened pieces of copper were treasures to be shown to the smaller children who were not allowed to leave their yards. Tasha had to constantly remind the kids that the train tracks were dangerous and not a place to hang out. But there was just something about that train that caught the imagination of these young boys. Maybe it was due to the fact that the boys watched the train leaving town, headed to new places and new adventures, which was something they all aspired to do someday.

The boys started participating in organized sports as soon as they were old enough. Boys in their neighborhood played for the Lamar Hornets pee wee football team. The Rodgers brothers also played for their uncle Rodney in AAU basketball. Another uncle, Michael Lewis, was a local high school star at Lamar Consolidated. Lewis went on to star in football for the University of Colorado Buffaloes before being drafted into the NFL. He then played for the Philadelphia Eagles and San Francisco 49ers. He was named All-Pro in 2004 and selected to the Pro Bowl that same year. The Rodgers brothers gained a lot of their football skills and acumen by following the career of their Uncle Mike.

Growing up in a small town such as Richmond and being involved in kid league sports allowed many of the guys who would eventually play sports in school to develop strong childhood bonds. The extreme competitiveness between Quizz and James rubbed off on everybody. Danny Moore was the coach of the Lamar Hornets when James and Quizz started playing organized football. He saw first-hand the coming of age of the kids who went on to be the stars on varsity football for the Mustangs. He remembers the kids not having much outside of sports. "The first time I saw James and Quizz they were both on the same bicycle coming up Collins Road to practice. This bicycle had no seat. James was sitting on the handlebars and Quizz was pedaling while standing up the whole time. It was quite a sight to see."

The kids gathered at City Park for pee wee football practice on Mondays, Tuesdays, and Fridays. The games were played on Saturdays. The Rodgers brothers were more competitive between themselves than they were with opposing teams. Moore remembers the brothers always trying to one up the other. "It was all about getting the football and if one scored the other was dying to answer."

Charles Cone followed Moore and had several years with Quizz along with future varsity teammates Jonathan and Charles Taylor and Sule Osagiede. The coach generally moved up with his team each year. They got them as eight-year-olds on freshman squad. Then they had sophomore, junior, and senior squads which took them through to eleven years old. It all depended on how old you were on September 1st, which was the cut-off date. Because of where his birthday fell, Quizz played two years on the freshman squad, once with Moore, and then with Cone. Moore moved up the next year along with James Rodgers and his age group.

Cone also got to see Quizz from day one of his football career and remembers how special the youngster was from the start. The kids growing up in small town Texas live to play sports because there really isn't anything else. Richmond was a typical small city suburb of a major city, Houston, but was far enough away to still have a small-town atmosphere. After coaching the freshmen for a while, Cone noticed that Quizz was always the first kid to practice. "I rarely beat him to the practice field even though I tried. He was also the last to leave. He didn't want practice to end."

Cone noticed some distinct ways in which Quizz acted that were not typical of other eight-year-olds. He was so dedicated. "I don't think he ever missed a practice. Very committed at such a young age. It became obvious that Quizz was head and shoulders above everybody else even though he wasn't the biggest kid there. He was by far the best athlete. But he was very nonchalant about everything even if he had just made a big play." Cone often gave kids rides home if they didn't have one and then pick them up on Saturday morning before the games. Quizz was always in full pads and uniform when Cone arrived. And his bed was always made before they left.

The twin cities funneled kids into the Lamar Consolidated Independent School District which in 2007 included three high schools: B. F. Terry, Lamar Consolidated, and John and Randolph Foster. Foster was relatively new in 2007. Lamar and Terry had a long-standing rivalry that was both friendly and ultra-competitive due to the fact that the kids all grew up together and played youth league sports together. Lamar Consolidated High School consisted mostly of kids from Richmond but also some from a small portion of Rosenberg, the City of Kendleton, and parts of unincorporated Fort Bend County such as the developments of New Territory and Greatwood.

Former Lamar coach Mike Zierlein grew up in Richmond in a football family with a father as a coach. Mike attended school at Lamar Consolidated, and he later coached the Mustangs. He always had a certain fondness for his hometown. "The community has been the same since I grew up there in the 70s and 80s, with different sections of different affluence. When I was in school the football team was a big deal. Then they stopped winning and the football team lost its popularity." Local support for the Mustangs had waned in the 90s. Zierlein's first year there as a coach was 2003 and Lamar went winless. The program had really taken a downturn and when Lydell Wilson took the reins they had about forty kids in the program. On road games in particular one could easily count the number of fans in the stands. As the program gradually improved the next year, attendance picked up, and the following three years they had very large turn outs.

Zierlein remembered hanging out in his neighborhood as a youngster with little to worry about compared to the problems in the bigger cities such as Houston. "The people in Richmond-Rosenburg were generally good people. There were some areas that were tougher than others but, for the most part, it was a community that looked out for each other and knew each other well." In Zierlein's first year at Lamar he was a floater, meaning when he taught he bounced from classroom to classroom. One of the teachers there was someone he had worked with at Bay City. On one of his first days, she told him about these two smaller players who would be in the program who were great youth league players. "She didn't have any kids that age, so she basically knew about the Rodgers brothers from word of mouth. It definitely had me curious."

The student body at Lamar Consolidated was very eclectic. They had several different races with different financial and social backgrounds. There was a strong Nigerian presence on the team. Sule Osagiede, Chuck Obi, Andrew Nwaogwugwu, Andrew Okokhere, Jeffrey Okonye, and Prince and Presley Godson were all of Nigerian descent. Many of the Nigerian families lived in nearby New Territory. Their young men were known to be disciplined, respectful and hard working. At Lamar Consolidated there was a mix of Latino, white, and African American boys, and they all grew up together which resulted in a strong brotherhood by the time they all reached high school.

Lamar coach Pet Peloquin remembered when the kids were getting close to high school age, they had already started talking about what they were going to accomplish. The youngsters had aspirations from the start. They had plans. "When I first started paying attention to James and Jacquizz and their bunch, they were already getting competitive." Peloquin had a Ford Ranger. and somebody asked for a ride home one day. Then the next time there were two, then three. Soon he had the whole truck bed full of kids back when that was still allowed. And when it rained it was a contest to see who got in the cab because there could only be two others with the coach. He heard their conversations. They had their eye on the prize.

As they got older, the Rodgers brothers practically lived at the high school field house. They would just as soon be there as at home sitting around doing nothing. And if James and Quizz were in the weight room then everybody else had better be there. It was more than just competition. It was manda-tory in their minds. It was about commitment and showing that you cared as much as they did. Anything less would not be accepted. Peloquin remem-bers that the coaches didn't have to say anything. "The kids set the bar them-selves. We knew we had something special happening with that bunch."

Sports ran deep in Tasha Williams' household. But academics came first. Although James Sr. was not active in supporting his sons' efforts, the two uncles were there to make sure James and Quizz stayed involved. During the boys' elementary school years, they had Michael Lewis to model their athletic achievements after. Michael was also being helped along by Rodney, who was older and had played college hoops in Seguin, Texas at Texas Lutheran College. After college, Rodney returned to the Richmond-Rosenberg area where he was around to assist a young Michael in school and sports. Like most young men, Michael was more interested in non-academic activities than scholastic endeavors. Rodney encouraged him to pay more attention to his grades and life beyond Lamar Consolidated Mustang football. Soon, a young Michael became an honor roll student.

Lewis recalls his youth in the Richmond area. "Coming out of small-town Richmond you have to be very serious about taking care of business to make it to the college level in athletics. In junior high, academics were not a high priority for me. When I realized that academics were more important than athletics, I got serious about school. I knew football was my ticket to college, and once I got to the University of Colorado, I wanted that degree." If the NFL had not worked out for Lewis, he still had that diploma. He graduated in three years. This is what he wanted James and Quizz to understand. Academics would always be priority number one. But athletics was a means to get a scholarship. Making good grades was always number one.

Lewis was drafted after his junior year at Colorado, entering the National Football League with the Philadelphia Eagles. After Lewis left Richmond, Texas, it was up to their Uncle Rodney to encourage the Rodgers brothers both on and off the field. Once he became a pro, Michael joined his older brother Rodney in supporting the Rodgers brothers financially. Said Rodney: "For Michael and I both, it was the same idea. We needed James and Jacquizz to excel both on and off the field. This was as much about them being successful in the classroom as it was on the football field or the basketball court." The brothers were taught about the importance of getting a college education through being excellent in sports. There was not a lot of money laying around for college for two kids.

Rodney never missed their games. But, more importantly, he monitored things in school. His and Michael's support was directly tied to classroom performance. "We supported their athletics, but rewards were only given for grades. And we were going for As." One time, Quizz came home with a C grade. Tasha let Rodney know. He told Quizz, going forward, until further notice, the first two hours at home after school would be spent at the kitchen table studying.

One afternoon Quizz's buddies called and wanted him to go hang out. Rodney found out and headed to his sister's place. "I showed up and Quizz said he was headed out. I told him it looked like he had a decision to make. He challenged me and I said 'Oh, you're a man now.' He thought about it. It was one of those moments in life when he really needed to think about what he wanted most. It was not a democracy with me or my sister. He sat down and started studying. I told him not to make me do this again." Rodney gave his sister credit for always backing him up. "It's so important for adults to be on the same page too."

Coach Tim Teykl led the cross-town rival B.F. Terry Rangers. Teykl saw the potential in both Rodgers brothers early on. "Prior to their junior high school years, they were already making somewhat of an impression through their athletic abilities." Ft. Bend County had a pee wee football league that included the Rosenberg Roughnecks and Lamar (Richmond) Hornets. Teykl remembers first seeing James and Quizz when they became Hornets. In the pee wee rivalry, the Rodgers brothers were already excelling against the competition, even sometimes against boys one to two years older than them. It was obvious they had strong family support even though their father was in prison on drug related issues.

Teykl was always impressed with the Rodgers clan. "Those Rodgers boys had strong family support. Not just men such as uncles Rodney and Michael, but also female support such as mom, aunts, and grandmas. Their family provided a strong, influential structure on all fronts: academic, athletic, work ethic, accountability… it was quite impressive" recalls Teykl.

James Rodgers acknowledges the help he and his younger brother received from the male figures in their lives. "I would say Michael was definitely influential in our lives because we grew up watching him play football during his time at Lamar. My other uncle, Rodney, is the guy who impacted us the most. Just making sure we stayed busy, stayed on top of school, and adding that discipline factor in our lives that we needed. He was very instrumental in molding the two of us into the men we are today.

Coach Wilson knew the Rodgers were the right type of young men, along with the aforementioned strong Nigerian presence and others, who could become the solid nucleus of a winning football program. He needed the kids to buy in to what he was preaching. Running back Derrick Davis was on varsity in 2005 and saw the program turn around quickly once the kids started buying in. "When I was a junior, we were better than the record showed. We just could not finish games." The team lacked discipline in certain areas and lacked heart. Once everybody bought into the program the coaches put out, they were not to be messed with, period. The Mustangs went 2-8 in '04 and then improved to 11-1 in 2005, losing to Houston Yates in the regionals.

Part of that improvement was definitely the changes instituted by Wilson. But there also was the addition of players such as the Rodgers brothers and Sule Osagiede. Davis saw it this way: "It was a mixture. You had crazy competitors like James and Quizz. They simply made everybody better. James held teammates to a higher standard." Coaches Wilson and Zierlein came in and immediately improved the offense. And they had guys like Levar Brown and Jarvis Jones making plays on defense. Osagiede was the proverbial icing on the cake.

Coach Charlie Ayro picked up on the vibe that was developing soon after his arrival in 2004 after being a Graduate Assistant at McNeese State

University. "The culture was established when Quizz and Quon (James Rodgers) came on the scene. And also, DJ Smallwood and Sule Osagiede Those kids were so competitive, even against each other. Nobody got cut any slack, not even in practice. Friends would be in each other's face talking it up. Sometimes we had to calm them down. Sule and Quizz saw every practice as a personal challenge."

The players noticed early on that the new high school head coach was coming around watching them play. Linebacker Carlos Becerra remembers seeing Wilson soon after he arrived. "Wilson showed up for the seventh and eighth grade games. We thought seeing the varsity head coach was pretty cool." On one school evening, the head coach showed up for the seventh-grade game. He was searching for this special running back the kids referred to as "Quizz". On the first offensive series, Wilson watched this short runner who was gashing the opposing defense for big yards. He kept scanning the Lamar sideline looking for the stud running back responsible for all of the hype. Nobody on the sideline seemed to fit the description he had developed in his head.

Finally, Wilson's curiosity got the best of him. He turned to a middle-aged gentleman behind him and inquired as to where the Rodgers kid was. The man behind him happened to be Rodney Williams.

Wilson: Excuse me sir, which one is the Rodgers kid?

Williams: The running back.

Wilson: The little guy?

Williams. He's short but he ain't little. He's the best player on the field every night. And tomorrow night his older brother will be the best player on the field too.

At this point Quizz took a handoff and accelerated through the hole. The big middle linebacker from the other team met Quizz head on. The much taller kid knocked Quizz down before falling backwards on his rear. Quizz put his hand down to keep his balance and was quickly up and running. He made a couple of cutbacks and hit the sideline. He was gone for the touchdown, outrunning everybody to the end zone. The defenders had also become spectators, watching Rodgers do the incredible… as a seventh grader. Wilson sat and stared. He turned to Rodney Williams and, with a smile, shook his head in disbelief. Williams was beaming with pride. "That's my nephew, Coach Wilson. I'm Rodney Williams. Nice to meet you."

From that point going forward Wilson made sure to keep tabs on his two budding stars. The days and weeks seemed to crawl by as Wilson waited for James Rodgers' class to graduate to high school. Guys like Levar Brown, Jarvis Jones, Dylan Clark, David Banks, and Sule Osagiede were shaping up to be stellar athletes. Wilson saw the pieces of the puzzle begin to come together right before his eyes.

No one could blame Wilson for being in a hurry. Lamar Consolidated had gone 3-27 in the three years prior to the arrival of the Rodgers brothers to varsity football. Wilson would one day claim the two brothers "resurrected the soul of a community." The excitement was obvious with the Rodgers brothers on the field, as every home game was a sellout. It was amazing looking up into a packed high school stadium where the good seats were taken well before game time. A once-moribund program was now the talk of the town. A community was feeling some long lost pride.

As the time neared for the brothers to start high school sports, anticipation in the community was building. Wilson knew true change required everybody buying in to what he was building. Lamar had one of the longest losing streaks in the Houston area when Wilson arrived. It took some time for him to get the participation numbers back up. As time passed the momentum started building and it turned the situation in a positive direction. And the arrival of the Rodgers to varsity helped to change the mindset surrounding the football program. Finally, Wilson had players who were willing and talented enough to be molded into winners.

The hard work paid dividends in the fall of 2004 when James Rodgers was entering his sophomore year at Lamar and his younger brother was elevated to starter status by the third game. Quizz remembers not thinking much about it. "The coaches already had been watching me and they knew I could contribute right away. For me it was just that same old thing, playing football with my older brother."

Coach Ayro could tell this new group of kids were very close and loved being on the field together. "They all played sports together and against each other for their entire childhood. Now they got to show their stuff at the varsity level, and they couldn't wait." Wilson decided after the third game of the season the time was right to see what Quizz could do in the starting running back spot. Derrick Davis occupied the starting spot, and he was doing a good job. However, the coaches were itching to see what they had in their freshman prodigy. Wilson formulated a plan. He knew Quizz had that little something extra, and Davis could be moved to outside linebacker and start right away.

Coach Marcus McLemore was Rodgers' running back coach through the 2006 season. He inherited the responsibility of bringing Quizz along as a freshman and saw some similarities in his running style to some of the best who ever played the game. "Jacquizz had a very natural running style. I always thought of Maurice Jones-Drew because of his great vision and exceptional core strength." Many Lamar faithful also saw similarities to Barry Sanders because of how quickly Quizz could start, stop, and change directions. Quizz and his core of friends set the tone on the football field. But the fire burned hottest in Rodgers. He was relentless in his pursuit of that elusive championship. Winning means different things to different people. For Quizz, winning meant proving the pundits wrong about his lack of size, and to show opponents that this kid from the other side of the tracks was a force to reckon with. It was very much personal.

Linebackers coach Charlie Ayro also noticed that the kids remained close outside of school as well. He would sometimes give them rides after school or practice and they would stay at each others' houses often. "The coaches encouraged this as it brought camaraderie. And it wouldn't just be by position group. Defensive guys would hang out with offensive guys, linemen with receivers." All the parents knew all the kids. There was no such thing as a stranger among these players and their families.

The 2007 version of the Lamar Consolidated Mustangs was different from their predecessors. They had been hanging out in Richmond-Rosenberg together for a long time. They knew each other, knew each other's families. They genuinely liked each other, and they bonded through playing sports together. They just needed the right people around them to keep them focused and show them how to win, as in that certain coaching staff who could get the best from them. That whole process was set in motion in April of 2002 when the Lamar Consolidated school board was faced with a vacant head football coaching position. Their choice was Lamar Consolidated alum Lydell Wilson. The native son was coming back to where it all started for him, and he knew he had some work to do.

CHAPTER 3

LYDELL COMES HOME

I f Coach Wilson felt he had the right bunch in 2007, it was because of the groundwork he laid in 2002 when he landed the head coaching job at his high school alma mater. The Lamar Consolidated head coaching position came open following back-to-back losing seasons. Wilson had always dreamed of returning to his childhood hometown to lead the school he starred at before graduating in 1986. "The Mustangs of that era had a winning tradition" recalls Wilson. Prior to 2005 the Mustangs had only four wins in four seasons. While it may have appeared to some that the situation changed overnight, such was not the case. Wilson had a plan that was more of a culture change than a quick fix.

Wilson remembered when it was a big deal to wear the letter jacket. "It was our culture, a winning attitude about everything. We had our swagger, a confidence thing. At some point that all disappeared." After Wilson graduated high school, he played one year of spring football and three years of baseball at Stephen F. Austin in Nacogdoches, Texas. His first job upon college graduation was as a teaching aide for the Lamar Consolidated School District. After three years of doing that, Wilson decided to go back to school to get his teaching certificate.

The next three years were spent as the offensive coordinator for Stroman High School in Victoria. He then went to Ball High School in Galveston as the quarterbacks coach for three years. In 2001 he landed at Willowridge High School in Sugar Land where he was the offensive coordinator. But after only one year in Sugar Land the Lamar job came open. He applied immediately. He was the first person to get his resume in. He had always kept up with his old school and felt he knew the town very well having grown up there. Wilson wanted to restore the winning tradition he had experienced growing up in Richmond. The school board of LCISD hired Wilson on April 12, 2002, sixteen years after he had graduated.

Wilson's time at Stroman prepared him for the task at hand when he arrived back home at Lamar. Many considered the football program at Stroman broken in 1995. The staff that Wilson joined took it upon themselves to change the culture. Specifically, Wilson felt the kids needed some swagger, that confidence factor that was missing. If anything, Wilson's days as a player taught him that if one does not believe in himself, he's never going to be a winner. And it was not just a solo thing. A team needed to have a collective swagger.

Kevin Roehl played for Wilson at Stroman and remembers the changes. "Stroman was something like 0-49-1 when Wilson and those guys arrived. Wilson was very steady, he never got rattled. He had a quiet confidence that was contagious. It came out in the way he carried himself. He taught us swag with the way he dressed and his style of leadership. Plus, those coaches like Wilson and Zierlein were young, not much older than us. They could relate to us players on so many levels. But we respected them so much. They changed an entire culture. Stroman became a winner."

At Lamar, Wilson immediately realized the numbers were down. He needed the kids to get excited about football again. He initially started recruiting the hallways and held class meetings with all the boys in high school. Then he got them excited by showing them old videos of when Consolidated was good and the stands were full. He talked a lot about having school pride and wearing that letter jacket.

Coach Mike Zierlein remembers those days as well. "The turnaround was a combination of the things Lydell did and eventually the presence of the Rodgers brothers." Zierlein arrived a year after Lydell, and they formulated a plan to build a base and also make it fun. In addition to the Rodgers, they were blessed with three years of talented kids who also were willing to work very hard. They also had some kids transfer in who worked out and that was not always the case with transfers.

By 2004, Wilson was a very recognizable member of the faculty at Lamar. He and Zierlein would often walk the school halls looking for prospective players. The kids knew Wilson had a certain aura about him with the way he dressed sharply and how he carried himself. He tended to look a young man in the eyes and bend a listening ear, both of which were signs of seriousness and respect. He made every single boy feel needed. Wilson coming in gave the program instant excitement and credibility because he came from there and was part of a winning tradition that had gone away. Richmond-Rosenberg had a lot of people who grew up there and then wanted to raise their children there. They were all familiar with each other and remembered how much fun winning was when Lydell and his older brother, Roderick, played. Suddenly, the kids wanted to play football again and not roam the halls.

The plan worked magic in changing the students' outlook, and soon, there was a brand-new excitement around Richmond-Rosenberg. Part was the new coaching staff. Wilson brought in former Rice quarterback Donald Hollis to be the offensive coordinator. Marcus McLemore was the running backs coach. Jimmy Franklin came in to coach the defensive line. Jeff Mayfield and Mike Zierlein came on board in 2003. Zierlein took the controls as offensive coordinator and Mayfield coached the defensive ends.

Several holdover coaches remained as well, including some who had coached Wilson himself. Defensive coordinator Lane Wade coached Wilson as a Mustang, as did linebackers coach Gerald Thompson. Don Carter was in charge of the offensive line and Steve Hummel, who was also a graduate of Lamar, coached receivers. Brett Snuffin stayed on to coach linebackers and Pat Peloquin coached defensive ends.

Coaches would come and go between then and 2007. Ronnie Humphrey came in to coach running backs. Pat Mathews was brought onboard in 2007 to be the new offensive coordinator and also coach the offensive line. Charlie Ayro came along in 2004 and took over the inside linebackers. Wade continued as coordinator and personally handled the secondary. John Velasquez came on to coach the outside backers. Jason Calahan coached skill positions.

Matthews got there just in time. It was his friendship with Ayro that landed him at Lamar. Ayro and Matthews played together and then later coached together at McNeese State University. When Zierlein left to take the head job at Austin Akins, Ayro put Matthews in touch with Wilson. Ayro felt the addition of the new coaches had benefits beyond direct contributions. It became obvious that these new coaches were tough, no nonsense kind of guys. Just as important, they didn't know the players. They had no preconceived notions of who was who. It completely turned the team into an open competition.

They had certain ideas about who could do what, but the new coaches did not care what a player had done in the past. Coach Matthews in particular. During one game there were some words at halftime in the locker room about the O line not blocking. Coach Matthews got in Quizz's face and told him to stop dancing and hit the damn hole. It was an attitude changer for the team because they saw that everybody would be held accountable. There was no playing favorites. And it showed that the coaches were there to win.

Coaches Greg Kobza and Velasquez brought something new to the program as well. Wilson remembers the two coaches breaking down game film in a manner not seen at Lamar before. Wilson later saw that type of analysis grow in popularity and become more mainstream. "Those two coaches did things manually that *Hudl* does now." It all revolved around knowing your opponent's tendencies in most situations

Matthews had some knowledge about Lamar through his friendship with Ayro. He personally didn't know the legend of Jacquizz Rodgers. He had heard stories but didn't think much about it until he was around the young man every day. It didn't take long for Quizz to make a believer out of his new offensive coordinator. "What you saw in games did not compare to what we saw in practice with regard to Quizz. He was so intense, way more competitive in practice than other high school kids." But the coaches treated all the players the same. Matthews' attitude reflected a lot of McNeese tradition. Kobza came onboard and he was gritty and tough. Velasquez certainly didn't take any crap. The coaching staff was a tough bunch of guys who bonded over a burning desire to win.

One coach who some thought might not be there in 2007 was Wilson himself. The La Marque Cougars had quite a run in high school football in the years from 1990 thru 2006 and were the Division II defending state champions going into the 2007 season. In 2015 the Texas Education Agency closed La Marque's school district due to academic and financial troubles. The schools were annexed into the Texas City school district. It was a somber ending to one of the well-known eras of dominance in Texas high school football lore. It all started with a 1993 trip to the Class 4A State final. After that, La Marque was a perennial powerhouse.

In 2003 La Marque made another state title appearance under head coach Bryan Erwin, this time defeating newcomer Denton Ryan 43-35 in an all-time triple overtime playoff classic. La Marque continued to field competitive teams and advanced to the Division II title game in 2006 where they defeated Waco High 34-14. As often happens in Texas high school football, a larger school will cherry pick a proven coach, and that is exactly what happened with Erwin.

In the spring of 2007, a very attractive La Marque head coaching position suddenly came open after Erwin left for Flower Mound Marcus, taking his staff with him. Chris Jones interviewed, and La Marque also went after Lydell Wilson who had an elite resume and was well known for what he was doing at Lamar Consolidated with the Rodgers brothers. Wilson had a reputation for being a disciplinarian. The kids at La Marque caught wind of what was going on and, having already lent their support to Jones, protested. The superintendent, Ecomet Burley had other ideas. After receiving Burley's phone call offering him the job, Wilson had a big decision.

On a cool February evening, Wilson pulled out of the Lamar Consolidated high school parking lot. As he headed down Avenue H, he realized his mind was made up, and there were going to be some very disappointed people in Richmond when they heard the news. As he pulled into his driveway, he paused for a few minutes before turning the car ignition off. How would he tell Quizz, Sule and the others? Was he running from his own alma mater when they needed him most? The loss against Alamo Heights still haunted him. Graduation was about to rob him of most of his starters. 2007 would be mostly a year of rebuilding for the future. But who knew how well that would turn out? Were things really going to be better down the road in La Marque? So many questions with very few answers.

As he walked through the door, he was met by his wife, Pat. She knew the pursing of his lips meant he was chewing the facts of the situation. He was leaving his own people behind for one of the premier coaching jobs in the state. If only he could have been just a little more confident in this decision. Dinner went by silently. Pat knew her husband well enough to realize that more questioning was not what he needed on this night. The La Marque superintendent had made an attractive offer. Burley had assured Wilson that the school district was on strong footing and Wilson would have the full support of both the school and the community. Now all that was left to do was get the school board to approve the hire. A special meeting had been called. Burley was confident he could get the board to see his way.

Behind the scenes a small storm was brewing at 397 Duroux Road inside the La Marque high school. The Cougar players had heard the rumor: Lydell Wilson was coming from Lamar Consolidated to be their next head football coach. Had the school board not heard their pleas and the wishes of their parents? They had all made it known that Chris Jones was their man. No way they would ever play for Wilson. Phone calls were made. The entire team would sit out the season. These were the defending state champion La Marque Cougars! There was no way this town was going a full season without football.

As dinner wrapped up at the Wilson household, all that was left to do was wash the dishes and wait for that ominous phone call. Wilson no longer knew exactly how he felt at that moment. The mix of emotions had him pacing around the house looking for something, anything that needed doing. Surely there was something that he had been meaning to do. Finally, at 10:30 that evening, Wilson couldn't take it any longer. Why hadn't they called?

He reached Burley at home. The school board had bent to the wishes of the players and parents. Wilson was out, Jones was in. Wilson sat with the phone in his hand, not quite sure what to say. His body stiffened and his eyes narrowed. The superintendent mumbled something about being bothered by the fact that Wilson felt he needed to discuss the proposition with his wife first, and overall, just didn't seem enthusiastic enough about the position. As he hung up, Wilson immediately began to reconcile the situation. He had Quizz. He had Sule, Carlos, Chuck, and DJ. Those were really his guys anyway. Fate, it seemed, was keeping Wilson in Richmond-Rosenberg.

After he placed a call to Dr. Thomas Randle, the LCISD superintendent, informing him he would not be leaving, Wilson set out to finish his goal and dream of leading his own high school to a state championship. The native son was staying put. His players were also aware of the rumor circulating the high school, and they were none too happy about it. And neither were the citizens of Richmond. For too long their football teams had lived in the shadows of powerhouses such as La Marque and Texas City. Finally, they were fielding competitive teams and now the competition wanted their coach.

Defensive end Deante Ester heard the talk amongst the players about hoping to meet La Marque in the playoffs in '07. The rumor of Wilson possibly leaving had everybody upset. At the time that was the biggest fire lit under the team. Nobody wanted him to leave. He was Lamar's coach. He changed the team, changed the way they felt about themselves, and he instilled confidence. When word got out it created problems for both the schools involved. There was, of course, a high likelihood that the two teams could meet in the playoffs in a bi-district contest. Lamar was favored again to win their district and La Marque would be competitive in a district that included good teams from Friendswood, Dickinson, and Texas City.

The thought of meeting La Marque was in the back of their minds all year. Win district first and beat La Marque in the playoffs. It became the most anticipated game of the year. In the end, Texas City won the district title and Dickinson, which beat La Marque 43-22, was slotted for round one of the playoffs in Division I against the Mustangs. La Marque slid into the runner-up Division II slot and played El Campo who they routed 31-6. However, the following week in Area play the Cougars were upset by Lumberton 24-21. Jones resigned from the La Marque position in March of 2008 after being in the job just one season.

One common feeling the team had for their head coach was that he really cared about them and wanted them to be successful for themselves. Guys that are fifteen, sixteen, and seventeen years old are very perceptive about the adults around them. It does not take long to figure what people are all about. Coach Zierlein knew this all too well. "A coach has to genuinely care about the kids for them to trust him in order to get the best out of them. The kids know when a coach is not genuine. Each player has a different story and in many cases the coaches serve as their male role model in their lives. A coach may very well be the reason they become responsible adults. A common line among coaches is we want to develop good husbands and good fathers."

Defensive tackle Mason Quintanilla respected Wilson for how he was both on and off the field. "Off the field he was a real players' coach. On the field he was strictly business and expected us to perform at a high level every Friday night." Wilson knew if a player was focused and engaged. Before every game he would hold a team meeting and each position coach would walk to the front and ask each player a question for their specific position group and the assignment for any given play.

Tight end Dominique Briggs respected both Wilson's disciplinarian attitude and also his willingness to have an open mind during games. "Yes, we were a run it down your throat type of team for the most part. But with Wilson, at certain critical points in a game, his mentality was to think players, not plays. By that I mean he would be willing to choose a certain play for a certain player in a specific situation or time of the game. And he could be fearless. He might take a calculated risk based on his assessment of risk-reward. It kept things exciting."

Coach Charlie Ayro felt the team had the right chemistry between both coaches and players, and amongst the players themselves. The players had been a tight bunch for most of their childhood. "We really cared about them because they were such a joy to coach and were very coachable. I would sometimes give them a lift home and they were fun to listen to. They would open up about football and life in general. I could tell that DJ, Quizz, Sule, and Chuck set the tone."

In three short years Wilson brought a program back to respectability. He knew the time to strike was when the iron was hot. "We had a very unique bunch of kids starting with 2005. We worked our way up to making it all the way to the semis. A lot of people expected us to win it all in 2006. The truth is, though, the bunch we had in 2007 were closer."

The players not only respected each other but they also respected every single coach on the staff. The kids bought in because Wilson had walked a mile in their shoes. He grew up in the Heights area of Richmond, was successful in sports there. He had a connection with their folks. They believed in him. Wilson could say things to his players in a certain way and their parents would not question it. He had a total buy-in from everyone in the administration, school, and community. He was from the wrong side of the tracks and did something to improve himself. The players respected that. Every head football coaching job he got he was the first minority to be in that position in that district. It always appeared that he was held to a different standard than most.

Coaching that group of kids at Lamar made several things possible for Wilson. Not many minority head coaches had won a state championship in football in the Texas UIL. He won Class 4-A coach of the year honors. He was elected to the board of the Texas High School Coaches Association. "A lot of what happened to me personally was because of what that group of kids and that coaching staff and myself were able to accomplish together." Lamar Consolidated had their man and he was one of them. And yes, this too was very personal.

CHAPTER 4

PLAN B

Rebuild

The summers in the Gulf Coast region of Texas are hot and humid. There was no way to avoid it. The field house at Lamar Consolidated's Traylor Stadium was a beehive of activity. The returning Mustangs knew the drill. You showed up or were called out. The sacrifices necessary to win in the fall were made in the spring and summer. At the Mustang Crossing Apartments, Jacquizz Rodgers heard his older brother James turn their alarm off. Tasha had recently moved her young family into the small, three-bedroom apartment down the street from the high school. The kids slept two to a bed. With Tasha off to work early every morning, it was up to James and Quizz to get their days started. It was Tuesday morning and the brothers needed to get down to the high school where they met their uncle, Michael Lewis, to work out.

Lewis had just finished his morning session with his trainer. Lewis had chosen to spend the summer in Richmond instead of San Francisco where he had just become a member of the 49ers football team. After his time with his personal trainer, he met with his nephews and the trio often repeated some of Lewis' own workouts. Then the brothers came back in the afternoon to do the weightlifting portion of their workout and possibly some more running. Competition between the players during workouts had grown fierce this particular summer. A lot of this new attitude about working harder in the summer stemmed from their loss to Alamo Heights.

Around noon the other players started to roll in for some work with the weights. Linebacker Carlos Becerra was one of the first to arrive. Becerra immediately noticed some new faces. The word was getting around. Like most summers Becerra was involved in, guys were always competing in the weight room. But the summer of 2007 was different in that, although working out was voluntary, this current bunch had the attitude that it was mandatory. Accountability was taken to a new level. Nobody wanted to be that guy who was slacking. As he entered the field house, the smell hit him. That old familiar odor of a dated weight room. The faded carpet was worn, the weights were pitted from rust, and the concrete walls were losing paint except in places where pictures were hung. Former Mustangs such as Alan Faneca and Michael Lewis were among the stars of the past whose stares seemed to always be looking down on the players, sizing them up, and granting their approval or disapproval.

Becerra gazed at the reflection from the mirrors. These mirrors did not lie. This was not the super talented bunch from 2006. Those guys did not have to work as hard to win. They could often just show up and win on pure talent alone. At least they did until the day came when that no longer worked. The Alamo Heights memory was there every day, like a fog that would not lift. Becerra wondered how this bunch was going to accomplish what the '06 squad could not. He saw Quizz standing over the bench press, waiting to spot another player. Quizz too saw the reflection in the mirrors. He knew somewhere in there, in this building, amongst this bunch, were the answers. Quizz spurred his guys on. "The competition in the weight room was a result of the desire to win. You had to start somewhere. Maybe start by winning in the weight room and then go from there," recalled Rodgers.

Quentin Palmer remembers another topic of conversation in the weight room as well. The team before them was supposed to win state. "Now our group had a large chip on its shoulders because people were writing us off. All we had heard was how the team would be downgrading in talent at almost every position. And most of those positions were open still." The coaches themselves did not even know who their starters were going to be.

Linebacker coach Charlie Ayro sat in coach Wilson's office and surveyed the scene. He echoed Palmer's concerns. "I told Wilson that we were going to have guys start for us in 2007 who had never been starters before. I told Wilson we might win six games during this rebuild." The coaches had no way of knowing how the new players would respond or what kind of team they were going to be. Suddenly the banter in the weight room quietened.

Something was up. Wilson nodded to Ayro who quietly stepped into the doorway to take a peek. Quizz was on the bench press, going for a personal record (PR). The room waited, some out of curiosity, some knowing the message that could come forth. Quizz steadied his breathing and firmly lifted the bar. As he lowered the weights, every muscle in his thick chest tightened. He powered the heavy load back up and racked the bar. The room remained silent as the moment sunk in. Now the question was … who's got next? The remainder of the week would be about nothing other than PRs. More competition. Ayro turned back to catch Wilson's wink and a smile.

Wilson probably worried the least of anybody. He knew as long as they had Quizz, Chuck, DJ, and Sule that they had a chance of doing well. And Wilson believed in himself and his ability to get his guys to buy in to what he was doing both on the field and off. Everybody lost something to graduation. An old coach told him over the summer that they would be okay. Kids would step up. What mattered most was their core group of leaders and getting every single player and assistant coach to buy into the program. Besides that, the kids coming up were more of a team, less individualistic. They were guys who could be molded. They rooted for each other. Their bond was unequivocal, and a lot of really good football teams across Texas would soon learn just how much this bunch cared.

Defensive lineman Deante Ester showed up to put his time in. He was especially sensitive to the talk that surrounded the team. He couldn't help but hear the whispers, the off-handed comments. Expectations for the current team had dropped significantly. As the summer went by the new group began to develop confidence because everybody was showing up and putting in their time. The commitment was there. The defensive guys were talking about the season to come, and how they were going to be better than the previous year when not being able to stop Alamo Heights had exposed some things.

The defensive guys realized that Alamo Heights had given everybody else the blueprint on how to attack Lamar. So they decided to work on certain aspects of their game. The defense knew that strength had never really been an issue. What they needed was better overall speed and conditioning. They needed all eleven guys on defense to swarm to the ball and be relentless on every play. Conditioning would be the difference. Ester took the lead. He told Clarence Ward, Osagiede, and anybody else who would listen that they needed to kill with speed and tenacity. They would keep hitting them until they got tired of it, and then hit them again. It was music to Osagiede's ears.

Ward decided one afternoon it was time to shake things up. If speed was going to be the difference maker, then there was only one way to attain it. "Us defensive guys started jumping into running drills with the running backs and receivers. After a summer of that, we knew our speed was going to cause a lot of problems for opposing offenses."

The mix of offensive guys with defensive ones sometimes made for some humorous moments, especially anytime the flamboyant Ester was involved. After hitting the weights, Ester sauntered out of the field house onto the playing field. Quarterback DJ Smallwood had everybody running pass routes. Ester fell in for a turn.

Becerra: Uh, 'scuse me D, but this is receivers.

Ester: Man, y'all ain't got these moves.

Smallwood: You want the long ball? You wanna go deep?

Ester: Just put enough air under it if you think you can get it there.

Smallwood: Ball will be there.

Smallwood, simulating a live snap yelled "Go" and dropped back, all the while with a grin on his face. He launched the ball deep. While everyone watched, Ester began to lumber down the sideline. Suddenly, he got a bead on the ball and kicked in the afterburners, making a smooth catch in the end zone. It was a catch that would make NFLers Larry Fitzgerald or Odell Beckham Jr. proud. The snickering stopped.

Smallwood: D got some speed…

Jacquizz Rodgers was on the track that surrounded the football field. He ran 100-yard sprints and was drenched with sweat. His chest heaved as he tried to suck some oxygen out of the blanket of humidity. He was following a routine set up by his Uncle Mike. This was Quizz's time, and this was his sanctuary. He ran until his legs no longer complied. His Uncle Rodney knew that overall speed had always been one thing that had haunted his nephew. "Quizz never trusted his speed. He was a cut-back runner. The thing is, he always had plenty of speed." The other players watched out of the corner of their eyes as their star running back toiled under the mid-day sun. It was inspiring.

With James leaving mid-summer, Quizz was now on his own. Here again his uncle Rodney stepped in to help, along with Michael, to keep Quizz on the right path. Williams remembered the change. Before James left for college, he always was the one to get Quizz up for workouts. After James left, Rodney challenged Quizz to figure out who he was: Was he a follower or a leader? He could no longer rely on his older brother. Williams saw his nephew step up his commitment. "Quizz took the challenge and pushed it out to his teammates."

James was less concerned than his uncle Rodney. He knew Quizz had to become a leader and was confident in that because Quizz was so competitive. "Considering the fact that the 2006 team was probably more talented, I figured Quizz realized that he needed a better plan. This new bunch was closer as a team, and I felt like a lot of that came from Quizz stepping up his role." Quizz's personality made him more of a leader by actions than by words. His teammates saw his workouts with his uncle Mike and knew Quizz had taken things to a whole new level.

Lewis felt he also needed to challenge the younger nephew. "I had just signed with the 49ers and I knew I was going to continue to miss a lot of Quizz's games. I wanted to prepare him in every way possible." Quizz's workouts mimicked those of his uncle. He was training at the level of an NFL player. It didn't stop there. The two talked about school and the need to get a scholarship. Grades were the number one priority. Good grades opened doors. College degrees opened doors. When the time came for Mike to leave, he knew his nephew was ready to have a big senior year. "Some folks might have thought I was putting too much on his plate. I challenged every inch of him. I wouldn't be there. I felt the greatest love I could give my nephew was to set the bar very high. I wanted success for him as much as I wanted it for myself. I knew he respected me, and I knew I had his full attention. So I laid it all out there for him."

This "plan" was more than just a means to win a state championship. This plan was also a way to get Rodgers out of Richmond-Rosenberg and into a Division I program so he could follow in his Uncle Mike's footsteps and be a college athlete. Rodgers soaked it all up like a sponge. His uncle had become an honor roll student and then graduated from the University of Colorado in only three years. Quizz had the perfect template for success right in front of him.

With James gone to college, things were somewhat quiet back in Richmond. Tasha Williams made sure her two boys kept in contact. The brothers talked frequently. "They had always been each other's best friend. Their bond was irreplaceable, and they were each other's biggest fan and biggest critic." James understood his brother's disappointment after the semi-final loss. Quizz had unfinished business.

Their uncle Rodney also had worked to make sure his nephews developed a strong relationship. "We always kept them together in sports. Quizz played a year early in pee wee football so he could start with James." When Rodney was asked to coach James' youth summer league basketball team, he agreed only if they allowed Quizz to be on the team. Now James had left for Corvallis and Quizz was without his brother for the first time ever.

As the summer passed, it soon became time for a competition that was becoming popular in Texas. The annual 7 on 7 tournament was starting up. In 7 on 7 competition there is no blocking or tackling. It was created mostly for developing the passing game while allowing for some friendly competition. It evolved into a major tournament with the likes of Kyler Murray being a marquee name during his time as quarterback for Allen High School. The Mustangs fielded a competitive bunch and even surprised themselves. Palmer recalled the benefits of participating in the tournament that summer. "It was a great early bonding experience for many of us who had not started on varsity before." The Lamar contingency got within a game of making it to the championship. It was an eye-opening experience and one that gave them some confidence as a group. They learned they could be very good defensively as well after they shut down some high-profile offenses.

For sophomores DD Goodson and Jamal Williams, the 7 on 7 experience was invaluable. Goodson used that time to become familiar with the varsity guys. For the two sophomores it was a huge opportunity. The tournament was where teams built pass game chemistry. Goodson and Williams also learned that the speed of the game at that level was much faster.

DD's older brother, Justin, also participated in the competition. He saw some changes occurring. "By the time we got back to our workouts at Traylor we had become this tight knit group. What started off as competitiveness between ourselves turned into a group that, once we got into sync, it became all about winning as a team."

Linebacker Cory Green was unable to get to the high school over the summer. However, Green understood the importance of working out as his teammates were doing. He lived too far from the school to make it to the field house, so he did his own thing. Green lived in a small town, Kendleton, located about thirty miles west of Richmond-Rosenberg on Highway

59. He found a job working at a summer camp in Sugar Land as a teaching assistant. He also carried a huge chip on his shoulder from the previous season's loss to Alamo Heights. So he looked for a way to get his work in. "There was a small college, Bay Ridge Christian College, that had shut down. I discovered that they had a small gym, so I got permission to use it. They gave me a key for the summer."

Meanwhile, Coach Wilson and his staff, some who were new to Lamar Consolidated, were busy trying to figure out what their 2007 team would look like. As the coaches looked at the depth chart, they found many holes and uncertainties. It was almost like starting over. Smallwood and Rodgers were set in the backfield. Osagiede was their defensive captain from his linebacker position. They moved Carlos Becerra from corner to outside linebacker. After that it was mostly up in the air.

Smallwood was set at quarterback. The junior signal caller had spent the spring and summer rehabbing his knee after surgery following the '06 season. He had injured the medial collateral ligament the summer going into his sophomore year and played the entire year with it. He had surgery in the spring. By the time he got to the start of the '07 season he was feeling better about it, and it was just a matter of getting his strength back. The junior signal caller knew he would have to pick up the slack created by the loss of such offensive threats as James Rodgers. Smallwood merely had to be serviceable in 2006 with so much proven talent surrounding him. Now, in 2007, he would be responsible for carrying a greater portion of the offensive load, even with Quizz in the backfield.

Smallwood was born in Richmond, Texas on November 10, 1990. Like most kids in Richmond, he attended Deaf Smith Elementary, T L Pink Elementary, and Wessendorf Middle School prior to Lamar Consolidated Junior High and High Schools. And also, like many of the local kids, DJ started his football career at the age of nine years old, suiting up for pee wee football as a Hornet. Smallwood's size made him a good fit at tight end.

Then childhood friend Marcus Martinez encouraged Smallwood to join the Pecan Grove Gators where DJ transitioned to quarterback. "I played street football with Marcus at Pink Elementary, and he remembered that I had a good arm. So he and his dad introduced me to the Gator coaches and persuaded them to give me a try at quarterback."

In the sixth grade, Smallwood led the Gators to a Little League Super Bowl championship, a sure sign of things to come. After the Gators, Smallwood went into seventh grade football and quickly established himself as the starting quarterback. The same happened in eighth grade. As a freshman, Smallwood's talent elevated him immediately as the starting quarterback for the junior varsity. His sophomore year in high school was his first chance to lead a very talented varsity program, something that was not lost on the underclassman. "I knew I was surrounded by some D-1 talent. Jarvis and those guys were getting college offers. They had built a winning program and expectations were high. After a few games I knew I was going to be okay."

Smallwood took to following NFL quarterback Brett Favre and decided the position was definitely for him. Favre's #4 jersey number was already taken by James Rodgers. After doing some research on the Green Bay Packers he learned about Vince Lombardi and Bart Starr. That's when he adopted Starr's #15 jersey. He has remained a Packers fan ever since. And much like Favre, a gunslinger himself, Smallwood learned to love throwing the long ball. For DJ it became "money."

Head coach Lydell Wilson watched with a careful eye as Smallwood grew up. For Wilson, the relationship with his future quarterback was personal. "DJ's father and I were best friends growing up. We played on the same Lamar Consolidated football team together. He lost his father to cancer while I was away at college. My mother and his grandmother were close as well. DJ was always the best athlete on the field until he got on varsity. He was surrounded by some pretty good talent. He held his own though, and he became a good leader. He had a really good understanding of what we wanted to do on offense. I believe he is the winningest quarterback ever at Lamar Consolidated."

Even though his father was not there with him in high school, Smallwood had plenty of family support. "I always felt my father was there with me in spirit. Plus, I was raised by both grandmothers, and they definitely made me tougher. And the community was close. People looked out for each other and each other's kids. There were plenty of grown-ups to go around."

Smallwood went into the 2007 season feeling he had unfinished business. He carried the Alamo Heights loss with him the entire spring and summer. "The Heights loss was humbling because we had breezed through people up to that point. We had all these great D-1 guys and then that happened. It was eye opening because we hadn't even thought about ever losing. I really had to step back and think about things." By the time Smallwood finished his high school career he had amassed a record of 36-5 as a starting varsity quarterback.

Rodgers saw this potential too. Jacquizz stated it all himself: "We knew all along that DJ was going to be our quarterback. We didn't think anything about it when he started as a sophomore. We knew he was the guy from early on, when he was young… we saw that he was going to be the one. It's what he was born to do… he was a natural."

Osagiede was firmly established after three years on varsity. But more than that, he was entrenched as the outspoken leader of the team. As phenomenal as Quizz was on offense, Osagiede was every bit his equal on defense. Unlike Quizz, Sule had the gift of gab. He never passed up an opportunity to offer an opinion, regardless of the subject. And when it came to competing, his performance more than backed up his rhetoric.

Prince Sule Viscount Osagiede Ogbeowenwenkon was born on July 3, 1989 to Wisdom and Jennifer Osagiede. He was of Nigerian descent and a member of the Benin Royal Family of Nigeria. His father was a Major in the US Army at the time. Like his Nigerian teammates, Sule was raised to be respectful and disciplined. He also happened to be very athletic. Sule was also very charismatic by nature. He was always smiling and could talk to anyone. And talk he did.

Sule's childhood was typical of most kids in the Richmond area in that he played pee wee football for the Lamar Hornets along with Quizz. He split time between his mother's home in Alief, a section of Houston, and Riverpark which was located just east of Richmond where his father resided. Riverpark had a large Nigerian presence that included the family of teammate Chuck Obi. Riverpark just so happened to be zoned into the Lamar Consolidated school district and, more specifically, to Lamar Consolidated High School. Sule was everybody's friend and easily the most popular kid in high school. He was a natural born leader. His personality and magnetism drew people to him and spurred his teammates to want to be winners.

Quentin Palmer admired Osagiede for his tenacity and character. "Sule was the epitome of the word 'leader.' On the field, he was amazing. Fast, strong, verbal, fearless, but most of all, he was a warrior. Nothing could stop him from reaching his potential on each play, not even a torn ACL. But it's what he was off the field that separated him from all the other great players on the team. Sule was 'that guy.' He was the face of the LCHS Class of 2008. He did not see color. Sule hung out with Blacks, whites, Latinos, Asians, and everyone in between. He was extremely smart. Teachers could not get enough of his huge personality. He had a gift for making everyone laugh no matter what they were going through. Every person that graduated in the 2008 class could have looked up to Sule in some form or fashion. He was such a balanced individual."

Jonathan Taylor, who played football with Osagiede from pee wee through varsity, saw the tenacity from day one. "During Spring practice junior year Sule got a concussion. They damn near had to sedate him to keep him off the field." Osagiede did not understand why he could not participate. His larger-than-life personality made him a natural as the eventual team leader. And his guys wanted to show their leader they were up to the task every single day, whether it was practice or real time.

Osagiede was put on the varsity team as a freshman. Initially the coaches used him over the center in what they coined a "nasty nose" in reference to the nose-tackle position. Sule often met the running back in the backfield at the same moment the quarterback was attempting to handoff the ball. He transitioned into the linebacker spot for his sophomore year. He was a natural from day one.

Lamar Consolidated hoopster Keenan Seahorn was two years older than Sule. Seahorn's younger brother, Jarrod, played football with Osagiede. Keenan watched his younger sibling and friends develop a very tight bond that included himself. "I was the older guy. My senior year I was their Uber before Uber. They were always together, and we would ride around in my Isuzu Jeep and freestyle rap." Keenan had a child when he was nineteen years old. Trying to attend out of state college and hoop while still taking care of business was difficult. Sule pulled him aside one time and told Keenan how proud he was of him for not giving up when there was a child to be responsible for. That was who Sule was. He cared about everybody. "To this day when anything 43 comes up I say What Up Suk" says Seahorn.

Osagiede suffered a knee injury during his junior year. It was the Anterior Cruciate Ligament, or ACL. He managed to play through the pain and helped the Mustangs get to the semi-final game against Alamo Heights. After the season he had surgery on the damaged knee. He then spent the spring of 2007 and part of the summer strengthening the knee. With so much senior talent gone from the defensive side of the ball, Sule knew he had to be 100% healthy if he was going to lead his Mustangs back to the level of competitiveness they had become accustomed to.

At 6' 0" and 190 pounds, Osagiede was a physical specimen. Even after recovering from knee surgery, he could run a blazing 4.5 second forty. It was his quickness that made him tough to handle by opposing offenses. He had natural linebacker instincts as well and would often "shoot the gap" as though he knew the play calling of the opposing offenses. His range was sideline to sideline. And when it came time to talk his team up, he was always ready. It all emanated from his natural love to destroy opposing offenses. He was the smiling assassin, the Benin Prince, and the Minister of Defense.

Rodgers and Osagiede had a special bond from an early age. Rodgers' mother, Tasha, remembers the young Sule. "He always had that outgoing personality. You just couldn't get past that smile. He was always at the house, and I loved cooking for the guys. But that boy could eat. It didn't matter what. Leftovers in the refrigerator? Sule took care of that. One time I discovered that somebody had been eating at my computer. That wasn't allowed. I started in on James and Quizz and then realized it was Sule. He was so lovable that I just let it go."

Quizz and Sule were built from the same mold when it came to competing. The football field was their domain and they made sure everybody knew it. The problem was that sometimes the two friends were a little too competitive between themselves. Sule's position coach, Charlie Ayro, remembers him being a challenge. "His motor was always running, and so was his mouth." Ayro assumed responsibility for Sule since he could be a handful. Sometimes Coach Wilson would tell Ayro to get control of his boy over there when Sule got too amped up in practice. He was a part of that ultra-competitive culture at Lamar.

The team was not the only place where there were new faces. Coach Wilson had lost his offensive coordinator, Mike Zierlein, who had taken the head coaching spot in Austin at Akins High School. Zierlein took coach Jeff Mayfield with him. Wilson had to quickly find a new OC and, as luck would have it, linebacker coach Charlie Ayro knew just the man for the job. Ayro put his old college buddy, Pat Matthews, in touch with Wilson. Matthews was offered the job in July of 2007, which did not leave him a lot of time to get up to speed. Coaches Greg Kobza and John Velasquez were also added in 2007.

One of the first jobs Wilson and Matthews needed to do was figure out the offensive line. The skilled positions were pretty much set. Said Wilson: "When you have the best running back in the state you sure don't want to drop the ball with his blockers." The coaches set about constructing a new O line from scratch. Some of the players who tried out had almost no real game experience.

Matthews had been forewarned. "We were very unsettled on the O line. They had a great group graduate the year before... guys like Jarvis Jones and Levar Brown." That left the Mustangs with no experience playing varsity and not many who had even started on the junior varsity. The situation instantly became an open tryout. The final lineup of left tackle Jose Pena, left guard Beny Bravo, center Alex Rohde, right guard Presley Godson, and right tackle Paul Alford did not take shape immediately. The situation with the O line remained fluid throughout most of the season. Matthews had his work cut out. The starting lineup depended on how each player did in practice during the week. The guys had to earn their starting spot on a weekly basis.

There were, however, two constants with that equation. Rohde was very intelligent and made all of the checks from his center position. Godson, at right guard, was very coachable and physically gifted. At 6'3" and 295 pounds, he became known for his pancake blocks, the ones that left the defenders flat on their backs.

For Rodgers, the offensive line scenario was never really a concern. He was well aware they had lost people, but that is football. He knew they would figure it out. As with most things to do with managing the team, Quizz never felt like it was any of his business. He trusted his coaches and his team.

Pena got in the mix at left tackle after the third game of the season. He started against Montgomery and it went well. He never felt nervous because he was blocking for the best running back in the state. "I knew if I could just hold my block for that one second, Quizz would make it work." It was a good feeling for all of the new linemen.

Initially coach Matthews had Clarence Ward playing both ways. Ward got sick for the Montgomery game and the coaches inserted Beny Bravo, which allowed Ward to focus solely on defense from there on out. The left tackle spot continued to be by committee for a while. Coach Matthews was looking for consistency. Jarrett Cobbin had quick feet which helped in the passing game. Matthews would sometimes move Paul Alford over to that side and he used his size and athleticism well. But Pena just kept coming and eventually he made the decision easy for the coaches because he continued to improve and refused to get off the field. That allowed Alford to stay at right tackle.

The coaches also had the offensive linemen work at different positions along the line. Then if a player ever had to fill in at another position it would not be totally foreign to them. The coaches eventually brought in sophomores

Cameron Garcia and Antoine Everett to make sure the team was two deep at each individual position. This move also created a lot of competition, which was exactly what Matthews and Wilson wanted. Matthews had one very tall order for his O line. Quizz was not to be touched until he had cleared the second level. The O line learned by watching film to never give up on a Jacquizz Rodgers run. They learned to hustle down field looking for second and third blocks. The whole thing worked because the players were selfless and cared only about winning.

Wilson, who was best friends with quarterback DJ Smallwood's father when they were young, would continue to invest ample time developing his quarterback and designing his offense around the talents of both Smallwood and Rodgers. Lamar was always going to be that run first physical style of offense. Smallwood gave them a legitimate option when teams overloaded the box to stop Quizz. It was a nice one-two punch.

By the time the 2007 season rolled around, Wilson felt he had the right chemistry with both his coaches and his players. For all the hoopla that surrounded the '06 squad, this current group showed they could come together as a group where it really was all for one, and one for all as Osagiede was known to say. Nobody would ever question that Rodgers was a once-in-a-lifetime running back for a high school coach. However, the number of weapons that became obvious on both sides of the ball had Wilson salivating.

The saying in Texas goes "make hay while the sun shines." If 2006 did anything, it showed the younger players that success can be snatched away at any time, and nothing is a given. Their time had arrived. A senior laden team knew they had one shot at redemption and glory. Their talent may not have been obvious, but their hunger and willingness to sacrifice were undeniable. Wilson saw every single position as a necessary component and would not allow any one individual to be a weak link. Competition was ever present throughout the season. As far as Wilson was concerned this '07 group was his real chance to catch lightening in a bottle.

Wilson decided that during the regular season the captains would consist of four seniors on any given week, two from the offense and two from the defense. One problem Wilson never had was intra-squad jealousy. With the "best player plays" way of doing things, the guys knew playing time was earned. And with the new coaches coming on board there were fewer preconceived notions about who was worthy of starting.

Defensive end Deante Ester never saw any type of jealousy or discontent.

"There were no issues about playing time. Each starter earned his way on the field. After what happened against Alamo Heights the previous year the players had something to prove and the only way to do that was to win." It helped that they were also each other's best friend.

Smallwood had these same sentiments. The loss against Heights affected the underclassmen. "Everybody came together, and it became about nothing outside of winning." They spent very little time talking or bragging about individual efforts. Much of this attitude was a reflection of Wilson himself. The head coach was consumed with having his team be the best prepared, both mentally and physically. He needed everybody on the same page.

Known as a disciplinarian, Wilson always kept boundaries and made expectations known. Smallwood felt his coach's wrath early on. During the quarterback's freshman year Wilson started talking to him about being the QB of the future. Then Smallwood showed up late to Spring practice one day of freshman year and Wilson made things clear. "Coach Wilson told me it would probably be best if I stayed on junior varsity until I could become responsible." Smallwood learned his lesson. "There just was not any room for foolishness with Wilson."

Linebacker Cory Green found it was easier not to test the head coach. He stayed out of trouble. He still had to do IG with the team from time to time due to others cutting up in the classroom. "For the most part, the players were well behaved and mature as a team. And very disciplined. We actually were the leaders around campus my senior year." They knew others were watching so they wanted to make a good impression. And their coaches were always watching as well.

Once the offense was set, Wilson needed to figure out the defensive side of the ball. Osagiede was the incumbent at inside linebacker, and he was the defensive captain. Carlos Becerra was moved from cornerback to outside linebacker. Ward occupied one of the defensive tackle spots. Defensive coordinator Lane Wade inserted Quentin Palmer and Andrew Okokhere as his starting corners. Wilson was delighted with the way the two first time starters responded. "Quentin and Andrew stepped up big time. We could not have asked for a better job done." Chuck Obi filled a hybrid position called a Rover. He was part linebacker and part strong safety. Steven Fleming stepped in to fill the big shoes left by the departure of James Rodgers at free safety. Fleming also became a bright spot in the 2007 season.

Cory Green earned his way into the other inside linebacker spot next to

Osagiede. That left the defensive line. Deante Ester and Andrew Nwaogwugwu started the season as the defensive ends. Colin Usen was the other interior defender next to Ward. Taylor Turner was the punter and shared place-kicking duties with Adan Gomez. As they prepared for their season opener at home against a very good Waller Bulldog team, the Mustangs appeared to be set on both sides of the ball. However, a storm cloud was brewing, and it eventually turned the start of the season upside down.

SECTION II

CHAPTER 5

LONE STAR FOOTBALL

n 2005 James and Jacquizz Rodgers were well known around town, and they had helped the Mustangs achieve a top 10 ranking in the state in football. But this was not the case just a new I'm years earlier. Lamar was near the bottom of their district for years. I have noticed over my lifetime that trends exist in Texas high school football. In the seventies it was teams like Brownwood who were perennial powerhouses. I always attributed it to their hall of fame head coach Gordon Wood. The same could be said for Vernon High School and their Hall of Famer, Leo Brittain. But generally, there are several common denominators with most winning programs. It could purely be a numbers game with larger city programs such as those around Dallas/Ft. Worth, Austin, San Antonio, and Houston.

There could be economic factors such as the boom-bust cycle of the oil patch. Midland and Odessa were two such cases. The Benson family chose to live in Midland and young Cedric attended Lee High School. He helped lead the Rebels to three consecutive state championships in the late nineties before becoming a college sensation at the University of Texas and thereafter in the National Football League (NFL). Midland's sister city, Odessa, whose oil field working families tended to live vicariously through their Permian High Panthers were chronicled by Buzz Bissinger in his bestseller, *Friday Night Lights*. Coach Gary Gaines' Panthers were often undersized and overmatched but the kids understood the important role the team played in their community. Their play often exceeded their talents.

The Midlands and Odessas gave way to some new large schools such as Plano in the nineties and later Allen High, both northern suburbs of Dallas.

The most recent emerging power in that area is Frisco. These large suburbs attracted families such as that of former Texas A&M star quarterback Kevin Murray. In 1984 Murray put his baseball career on hold to take over as quarterback at A&M. He led the Aggies to a huge upset win in the Cotton Bowl over Heisman Trophy winner Bo Jackson and the Auburn Tigers. The Murrays had a son, Kyler, who led the Allen Eagles to a record 43-game winning streak and three consecutive state championships. From there Kyler headed first to Texas A&M, and then to the University of Oklahoma where he won the Heisman trophy and was the first selection in the NFL draft by the Arizona Cardinals.

Sometimes demographics such as affluence tend to attract certain types of families, and, in the process, build and nurture winning football programs. One such area is Highland Park in the center of Dallas. The Scots football team has produced some great football players such as Detroit Lions quarterback Matthew Stafford who was the first overall pick in the 2009 NFL draft. Stafford led the Scots to a 59-0 drubbing of Marshall for a state championship in 2005.

More recently the Scots were led to back-to-back state titles by quarterback John Stephen Jones, son of Stephen Jones, whose father is Dallas Cowboys' owner Jerry Jones. It does not take a stretch of the imagination to see how football might be a priority at a school such as Highland Park. Add into this equation the fact that the school has managed to keep legendary head coach Randy Allen, whose resume includes 376 wins in thirty-six seasons, and it is easy to see how the Scots keep cranking out dominant teams.

Austin is another city whose affluent neighborhoods have attracted families with talented sons. Westlake high school has produced such talent as Drew Brees and Nick Foles, two NFL quarterbacks who each have a super bowl win under their belts. The Chaparral's current head coach is former University of Texas quarterback Todd Dodge. After graduating from Texas, he made his way to the suburb of Southlake just north of Ft. Worth. He built a dynasty at Carrol High School. His son Riley Dodge quarterbacked the Dragons to a state title in 2006 and is, at the time of the writing of this book, the current head coach at Southlake Carrol. Todd returned to Austin to take the head coaching job at Westlake and won a state title over Denton Guyer in 2019. Westlake met Southlake for the state championship in 2021 in what became known as the "Dodge Bowl". It was the first ever father-son matchup for a state championship in Texas high school football.

Another affluent area of Austin that has risen to prominence on the football field is Lake Travis. The Cavaliers started an incredible winning streak in 2007 and went on to a state record of five consecutive titles in a row. It all started when former NFL quarterback Gale Gilbert decided to raise his family in the Lake Travis Independent School District. His son, Garrett, led the Cavaliers to their first ever state title in 2007 with a 36-34 thriller over the Highland Park Scots. Garrett was named first team All-state quarterback in Class 4A that year and was a member of the Dallas Cowboys in 2020.

The following year Gilbert again garnered a state title when Lake Travis defeated Longview 48-23. Gilbert left some big shoes to fill when he headed off to the University of Texas. The situation was handled quickly because former UT quarterback Robert Brewer had moved his young family to Lake Travis. Son Michael stepped right in, and Lake Travis did not miss a beat. Brewer did his part in securing back-to-back state titles before handing the keys to the Ferrari to another prodigy. Brewer had a stellar college career at Virginia Tech.

James Mayfield played college football for the Houston Cougars. He eventually moved his family to the Lake Travis area and son Baker attended school there. As a starting quarterback Baker led the Cavalier football team to a 25-2 record that included the 2011 4A state championship. From there, Baker started his college football career at Texas Tech before transferring to the University of Oklahoma. He brought another Heisman Trophy to the Sooners organization before becoming the first player taken in the 2018 NFL draft by the Cleveland Browns.

There were schools near the San Antonio area that were the benefactor of the numbers game, location, and good coaching. Such schools as the Converse Judson Rockets and the Cibolo Steele Knights had their time in the sun as state champions. Houston area schools also thrived on the football field at times. But a highly mobile population has limited its dynasties, with the exception of Katy to the West and North Shore to the East. Coach Gary Joseph has kept his Katy Tigers relevant for many years. The city of Katy recently built the $70.3 million Legacy Stadium where the Tigers now strut their stuff. The stadium seats 12,000.

Lastly, there is the Texas Gulf Coast whose landscape is dotted with refineries and factories stretching from Beaumont at the border with Louisiana down to Freeport. It does not seem that long ago that Beaumont French High School played a highly touted Odessa Permian Panther team to a 21-21 tie in the 1984 Class 5A state championship game. It was the last time the state would allow co-champions. French was subsequently folded into West Brook high school. One only has to glance at a map of the coastal area to see such dominant schools as the Texas City Stingarees, the La Marque Cougars, and the once mighty Bay City Blackcats.

More recently the dominant coastal school has been Galena Park North Shore. The Mighty Mustangs are coming off back-to-back (2018 and 2019) Division 1 Class 6A state titles. In Texas, that is the biggest and baddest classification in high school football. They won the same title in 2015. A combined campus of 4,775 students makes it the largest high school in the greater Houston area. The Port of Houston nearby and all those refineries around neighboring Baytown attract a lot of families. These families produce a lot of sons, and all of those sons are funneled into the football machine that is North Shore. Still there seemed to be something a bit more with these Mustangs.

I went online to get some answers and started talking to folks in Meechie Davis' Texas High School Football chat group. I found that with North Shore there was tremendous community-wide pride. I heard comments like "North Shore is family" and "it's a great place to raise children because of the great communication between the schools and the parents." There also was mention of plentiful jobs and a working-class mentality. The high school players visit the middle schools, participating in pep rallies, and they also go to senior living facilities to play bingo and other games. And lastly, the program was elevated by talented head coaches David Aymond and his successor, Jon Kay.

So, all of these winning football programs have certain factors necessary to field consistently competitive football teams. Jobs, affluence, large student bodies, and great coaches all contribute to the winning formula. None of this was present at Lamar Consolidated High School when Coach Lydell Wilson arrived in 2002. The school was not close enough to the Houston area or the coastal region to benefit from the numbers game. Richmond-Rosenberg was not considered a particularly affluent area. Although the school had produced some good football players such as NFL Hall of Famer Alan Faneca, Earnest Jackson, and Michael Lewis, they had never made a grand splash in the post-season. All of which makes the story of their 2007 season all the more memorable.

CHAPTER 6

KICKOFF... GO TIME

The 2007 Mustangs season started with five Pre-district games followed by five district games. Generally, teams use pre-district to figure things out and work out the kinks. Players are often moved around to different positions to find the best fit. Pre-district is the ideal time to build team chemistry. This was more important in 2007 than in previous years due to the heavy toll graduation had taken on Lamar following the 2006 season. Wilson and his staff were very much in search for answers in most aspects of their team. These answers needed to come early so they could be ready for the "second season" that is district play. All that really matters in Texas football is doing well in district play so that a team can advance to the state playoffs. But any coach worth his or her salt knows that bad play in Pre-district tends to carry over into district play.

The Mustangs opened their season at home against a tough Waller Bulldog team at Traylor Stadium. After coming off a spectacular season the fans in Richmond-Rosenberg were interested to see what this revamped squad could do. They still had Jacquizz Rodgers toting the ball. They had four-year starter Sule Osagiede on defense. And, they had DJ Smallwood under center with a year of varsity football experience under his belt. There were unfamiliar faces everywhere else. Still, the stands were packed. For their part, the Waller faithful traveled well as the two towns were relatively close. The Mustangs opened the season ranked eighth by Dave Campbell's *Texas Football* magazine.

The Mustangs came out in their dark blue jerseys with silver numbers and their silver pants. The Bulldogs were in their visiting whites. Lamar's defensive front pressured Waller quarterback Jeremy Phillips early and often, leading to sacks and turnovers. When Lamar was on offense, Rodgers was effective early, and the Mustangs took a 25-7 lead into the half. Waller bounced back in the second half limiting Lamar to just one more score. The Bulldogs managed a late score and the game ended 31-14. The contest was a successful start to the 2007 campaign considering Waller was expected to be a tough out in their own district. Later that year Waller made it all the way to the quarterfinal round of the playoffs in Division II where they lost by one score to Dayton.

Next up was another home contest against the Ft. Bend Elkins Knights. The Knights were in Class 5A from nearby Missouri City. Early in the game, Elkins was plagued by mistakes such as fumbled snaps and interceptions. The Mustangs opened the scoring with a field goal by Adan Gomez. Later in the first half Elkins seemed to gain some momentum offensively as they drove down to the Mustang 25-yard line. The drive ended, however, with a Steven Fleming interception in the Mustang's end zone. Fleming was taken down at the Mustang one yard line.

Smallwood quickly went to work from the shadow of his own goal post when he found his tight end wide open over the middle. After collecting the pass, Dominique Briggs ran over and around several Knight defenders before he was run out of bounds at the Elkins 30-yard line. It was another example of Lamar's big play capability and the plethora of weapons Wilson had at his disposal. The drive ended with a nifty scramble by Smallwood who then found Travis Riedel open in the end zone for a touchdown.

Smallwood continued to frustrate the Elkins defense with his scrambling ability, which only left more space for Rodgers to operate. Rodgers scored from thirty yards out late in the half to put the Mustangs up 16-0. Mistakes continued to plague Elkins, including a fumbled punt at their own 25-yard line that Lamar recovered. Quizz scored again to put Lamar up 22-0. Midway through the third quarter Osagiede missed a tackle and came up limping on his left leg. He tried to make it back to the huddle but suddenly dropped to one knee. The training staff rushed onto the field to check him out. He walked off on his own but had a distinct limp. Rodgers was concerned.

Quizz: You okay, man?

Osagiede: Nah, man, it's just …

The linebacker slowly shook his head as his gaze dropped to the turf. Junior inside linebacker Justin Goodson finished out the game in Osagiede's place. On the last touchdown drive Becerra came up hobbling after catching a pass from Smallwood. He also did not return. Defensive end Andrew Nwaogwugwu was similarly limping at the end of the contest.

While it was a check in the win column, the game was costly for the Mustangs. The medical staff, which consisted of Dr. Jeffery Liang, a sports medicine physician, and team trainers Dennis Fyke and Lance Hale, was suddenly very busy. The news of Osagiede's knee injury was shocking. He had just rehabbed a repaired right knee in the Spring. Now he was thought to have an ACL tear in the left knee, an injury that made his return in 2007 questionable.

Becerra's injury was a severe high ankle sprain, and he was also sidelined for a while. Becerra caught a pass from Smallwood near the sideline and got rolled up on out of bounds. He missed the rest of that game and all of the next against Montgomery. He played the rest of the season with his left ankle nagging him but there was no way Becerra was going to miss his senior year.

In week three Lamar traveled to Katy, Texas to play the Mayde Creek Rams, another 5A school. In spite of the difference in classifications, Lamar tended to have success against 5A schools, and they expected this trend to continue against Mayde Creek. The game seemed to be going as planned through most of the contest as Lamar led 26-16 with under four minutes to play. The Rams faced fourth down with twenty-one yards to go from their own 3-yard line. Quarterback Will Handlin hit receiver Chris Davis down the sideline for a 43-yard gain and a precious first down at Lamar's three. Running back Chris West took it in from there for a quick score to close the gap to 26-23. The Rams were suddenly within a field goal to tie.

Expecting an onside kick attempt, Lamar coach Wilson put in his "hands" team. This meant having more guys in to receive the ensuing kickoff who were used to handling the football. The Rams kicker instead hit a line-drive down the sideline that took a crazy bounce in front of quarterback Smallwood. The quarterback was not normally in on kick-offs but was inserted as part of the hands team. He misjudged the ball when it took a crazy bounce. It went over his head into Lamar's end zone. Mayde Creek's Mason Hooper pounced on the free ball for a Ram touchdown. The Lamar sideline was stunned. The game ended with an improbable Ram 30-26 upset victory.

In the locker room, an exasperated coach Wilson sounded off. "That was not Mustang football. We prided ourselves on being just as mentally tough as physically. We prepared for those situations. We did not execute in a critical moment. We had to fix that immediately." Lamar also needed to get some guys up to speed until they could get their regular starters back. The loss made some wonder if this bunch of Mustangs were up to the task. There were obvious chinks in the armor. How they responded going forward would tell the tale.

The Mustangs rebounded the following week with a 46-28 win over Montgomery at Traylor. Rodgers had his way with the Bears from district 18-4A, scoring early and often. He also had a big night on special teams with several long runs on kickoff and punt returns. For their part, the new guys on defense stepped up as well as could be expected. Justin Goodson continued in Osagiede's spot and Charles Taylor filled in for the injured Becerra. Meanwhile, Smallwood's scrambling ability continued to play a huge roll in the Mustang's ability to move the ball. He hit receiver Chuck Obi for a 25-yard touchdown pass before the half that put the Mustangs up by three scores. The Mustangs came out in the second half and quickly went to work on offense. Rodgers had a sensational touchdown run of forty-five yards that included several cutbacks and an all-out sprint down the left sideline.

Having seemingly righted the ship, the Mustangs traveled to the Woodlands for another matchup with a 5A school. This time it was the state ranked College Park Cavaliers. Wilson knew College Park was looking for both revenge and a statement win against a ranked team, even if it was against his 4A bunch. The timing was not good according to Wilson. "We really needed a break to clean some stuff up and get some people healthy. The kids thought we could just show up and win because we were Lamar. College Park had bad intentions."

College Park had several offensive stars on its roster who wreaked havoc on opposing defenses. Receiver Trey Diller and speedy running back Djeale "Jello" Lyons both had big play capability. It was obvious to corner Quentin Palmer that, from the onset, the Mustangs were not mentally prepared for this game. "I remember telling teammates early on that it felt like we were going into a trap game." A trap game occurs when the better team either gets caught looking ahead or does not show their opponent enough respect. While the 2006 Mustangs could afford such a mistake, this 2007 version was not at that level at this point in the season.

College Park got out of the gate quickly. Diller returned the opening kickoff eighty yards to the Mustang 15-yard line. On third down, Cavalier's quarterback Chris Brennan snuck in for the score and College Park was up

7-0 only fifty-nine seconds into the contest. On their first possession the Mustangs went three and out. The College Park crowd was fired up. All week long, all the Cavalier defense had heard was how special Jacquizz Rodgers was.

Lyons also had heard the talk, and he did not appreciate it. Hearing about Rodgers motivated him all week in practice. Lyons wanted to go out and prove that he was just as good. Jello did that and more, finishing the game with 201 yards on just fourteen carries. Defensive end Deante Ester felt helpless watching Lyons run up and down the field. Ester was out with an arm injury. The previous Monday he had just gotten home from practice and there was an argument about his future in football. That turned into a fight and Ester was tackled through what was supposed to be a shatterproof glass table. The defensive end had extensive lacerations to his left arm. Ester could only sit and watch as his team took a beating. "Nwaogwugwu was struggling with his injury. Sule was out. Lamar was the walking wounded."

Defensive tackle Mason Quintanilla also had a freakish injury. During his junior year he sustained an accidental gunshot wound from a .38 caliber handgun. The bullet went through both of his legs. It bothered him all year. Quintanilla and his teammates could do nothing to stop quarterback Josh Parsons and Lyons as they ran the triple option to perfection. The Cavaliers went up 14-0 on a Parsons keeper with 6:25 remaining in the opening stanza.

The Mustang offense, for its part, did little to answer. They managed only two field goals in the first half. The Cavaliers took a 21-6 lead into halftime. Looking for a change in momentum in the second half, the Mustang offense came out firing. Rodgers scored quickly to cut the Cavalier lead to 21-13. But College Park answered right back with a seven play 66-yard scoring drive that included a big 33-yard run by Lyons. The Mustang defense had underestimated Lyons and it cost them.

The Mustang offense did not score again. For the night, Quizz was held to a pedestrian 101 yards on twenty-three carries. Smallwood had just fifty-six yards rushing himself, and he was held to only thirty-two yards passing. It was not a banner night on either side of the ball for Lamar. The Cavaliers added a late touchdown on another impressive run by Lyons to finish off the Mustangs 35-13. For College Park, the game was redemption for the beating they had received from Lamar in 2006.

Lyons was especially satisfied with his big night. "We came into the game with a tremendous chip on our shoulders because of the way they had embarrassed us the year before. It was more than just a pre-district game. It was almost disrespectful how much people talked about Quizz in my own school, my own locker room, even my own coaches. After that game I felt I had earned their respect. Practice was intense the week before. Everybody wanted that win for many reasons. We definitely had our 'Mamba' mentality going."

Diller finished the night with 166 all-purpose yards. Although it was a successful night for the Cavaliers, he never felt like he was looking at a defeated Mustang team. "They never got down. To be honest, they were better than the score. The game came down to a few plays as always, and we had the better results on all of those plays. In hindsight, I would say they used that game as a wake-up call."

The one person who was most disappointed was Quizz himself. James Rodgers remembers their conversations following two early season losses. James felt the turning point for Quizz was after that second loss. The brothers talked weekly, and James sensed a change regarding how Quizz saw himself and his leadership responsibilities. "Quizz knew he could not just sit back and watch the season go down the drain. He felt the need to start pushing guys. After some self-reflection, he was on a different level as a player and a teammate."

The second loss left many of the Mustang faithful feeling the season was headed south in a hurry. Had they lost their best shot the previous year? Was the toll graduation had taken on them finally catching up? It was a solemn locker room afterwards. Coach Wilson had already had "the talk" after the Mayde Creek loss. And now there was this disaster. Obviously, something more was needed. Still, Wilson knew he had the right guys to fix this. The core leadership gave him every reason to believe they could right the ship. Lamar had two weeks before the district opener against Bay City. Drastic times call for drastic measures.

Coach Ayro saw no reason to panic. Their guys were so competitive. He personally thought that seeing how the backup players responded after the losses they had sustained from the Elkins game gave them hope. "Our guys felt like you got lucky if you beat them. Some people might have thought the season was lost. But our guys had this incredible self-confidence that I always attributed to Quizz and Sule."

Coach Pat Peloquin took it one step further. "We went into the season with so little experience. Then we had all of those injuries and normally under the circumstances that would have been devastating." But what Peloquin actually saw happen was that all of the backups stepped up and performed very well even though the losses made some people think otherwise. That made Lamar suddenly a very deep team even if they were short on experience.

For Wilson, the silver lining was that, in the future, he could count on his bench at almost every single position. He had all of these guys who were unknowns going into the season. The rash of injuries forced Lamar to play guys before the coaches knew if they were ready. They responded exactly as one would hope. Lamar just needed to get everybody on the same page now. The coaches were already coming up with a plan for Monday and the following two weeks. They put the College Park loss behind them before they ever left the stadium. But the media did not, and, just like that, Consolidated fell out of the state rankings.

Two people who were not so quick to move on were Tasha Williams and her brother Rodney. As they walked to the parking lot, they met well-wishers who did not know quite what to say. The nervous smiles passed back and forth did nothing to hide the disappointment at what they had all just witnessed. As they approached Tasha's car, out of earshot of the other fans and parents, Quizz's concerned mother turned to her brother.

Tasha: What was that?

Rodney: Don't know. Glad Quizz is already set with Oregon State. We shoulda taken care of business and won it all last year. I don't know if the hunger is there with this bunch.

Tasha: He ain't gonna be happy about this.

Rodney: And he shouldn't be. They got two weeks to figure it out.

CHAPTER 7

DISTRICT

Rivalry and The Catch Part I

The Mustangs were still feeling the sting of their loss to College Park when they showed up for practice on the following Monday. Little did they know the coaching staff felt it was time to get everybody's attention. This team was better than what they had shown, and it was up to the coaches to get the best out of them. The coaches had spent all of Monday morning coming up with a game plan to motivate this squad. They left no stone unturned. Forget football for now. They needed an attitude adjustment.

Coach Wilson and staff came out to practice barking. Nobody was exempt from their wrath. They knew their guys, and they knew exactly what was needed to motivate them. Coach Wilson's motto of "best player plays" was taken to the next level. Now it was "the one who wants it the most plays." The team knew immediately that something was up when Wilson walked onto the field. For his part, Wilson was willing to break it all down to the lowest common denominator. "We had a total refocus. That two weeks changed the season." The coaches were so hard on the players that they did not understand what was happening. The players were disciplined for every little thing—talking in the back of the huddle, chin strap not fastened, and so on.

The great thing was that no one was exempt. Wilson remembers Quizz having to do IG. "We would stop in the middle of practice, and I would ask the other coaches, 'How many you got?' We would either do up downs for how many they had [mistakes] or we would go get weights from the field house and go up and down the field doing different exercises with those weights."

The players responded exactly the way Wilson and his staff expected them to. They got their head into the program Wilson was creating. They totally bought in once they realized what was going on.

It would have been totally understandable if Wilson and his assistant coaches had been sympathetic with their players. The team was dealing with so many injuries and new bodies trying to fill in and get up to speed on the fly. Nobody would have said anything if the coaches had come in on that off-week Monday and eased the kids back into things. But that is what separated coaches like Wilson, Don Byrd, Jack Welch, Claude Mathis, Chuck Caniford, and my own high school coach, Leo Brittain, from the pack. They knew if they made a young man a winner on the football field, there was a chance he could become a winner in life. The Lamar coaches came into that off-week Monday with pure tough love.

IG was a concept brought in by Coach Mike Zierlein. It stood for Improvement Group, and it was a technique to get guys' attention both on the field and in the classroom. It involved some strenuous exercises to make the players think about their actions and consequences. It worked very well. Coach Zierlein saw players mature under this plan. "We became one of the least penalized teams year in and year out. Plus, you could see guys maturing in the classroom, thinking before acting. It carried back and forth between the classroom and the football field."

One frequent participant to IG was quarterback Dylan Clark, who led the Mustangs in 2005. "I was a member of a 'frequent flyers' group and we did some insane exercises, like 200-yard lunges with a 45-pound plate held over our heads. We would bear crawl until the whistle, which sometimes didn't come for quite a while."

BAY CITY

The Bay City Blackcats rolled into Traylor Stadium on a warm October Friday night to meet the well-rested and re-energized Lamar Consolidated Mustangs. Not everybody was healthy though, as Osagiede was nowhere close to returning, if he would return at all. Carlos Becerra's ankle sprain never completely healed the entire season. Deante Ester missed all of district play with his arm injury. Back-ups were being plugged in everywhere, and district was the second season, the one that really counted.

The Blackcats, as previously mentioned, had a long history of winning on the football field. In 1983, the Vernon Lions went into the season with high expectations based on the prospects of James Dixon in the backfield. Dixon went on to thrive in the University of Houston's Run and Shoot offense with Andre Ware. He then had a brief stint with the Dallas Cowboys. His talent was undeniable. That season was Vernon's last year in class 4A and they expected to go out in style.

Vernon breezed through district play before running into their old nemesis, Brownwood, and Coach Gordon Wood. Vernon escaped a crazy finish to move on. They eventually met Lubbock Estacado at Shotwell Stadium in Abilene. The Matadors were a high-powered offense but were untested to that point. It was thought that Vernon would be a tough out with Estacado being a slight favorite. From the outset it was clear that the Matadors' overall team speed was a problem for Vernon, and the Matadors won easily. Next up was the state championship against the Bay City Blackcats who featured wideout phenom Hart Lee Dykes.

The Blackcats had been ranked number one in most polls all year based on their returning starters. The Matadors went into that championship with tremendous momentum after dispatching Vernon without much trouble. It was time to show the state of Texas how the boys from west Texas played football. Not since the days of Breckinridge, Wichita Falls, Dumas, and Gordon Wood's Stamford squads had there been many champions from north central and panhandle Texas. The Matadors were big, athletic, and had team speed to burn. Final score:

BAY CITY	30
LUBBOCK ESTACADO	0

Bay City made it back to the playoffs in dramatic style in 2000 when they won the Division I Class 4A title by defeating newcomer Denton Ryan 24-2. The following year they made it back to the finals, only this time losing the Division II Class 4A final to Ennis 21-0. They came back one more time to the final in 2003 to lose the Division I title to North Crowley 20-6.

Bay City came into their district opener after finishing 2-8 the previous season and missing the playoffs for the first time in eleven seasons. First year coach Danny Edelman had come onboard in hopes of restoring the Blackcats

tus as a perennial powerhouse. What they ran into was a Consol-
n that had just finished two weeks of hell followed by a restora-
pose for the 2007 season.

wideout DD Goodson had been moved up to varsity along with fellow
sophomores Antoine Everett, D'Vonn Brown, and Jamal Williams. Goodson
saw that things were not so rosy upon his arrival to the varsity squad. "The
varsity was coming off a big loss to College Park. The coaches were scrambling to clean things up and make sure certain areas were sound before district. Us sophomores walked into a storm. Coaches were not happy; players
were not happy."

The Mustangs completely overwhelmed the visiting Blackcats, scoring
often. They rode the strong arm of quarterback Smallwood who went eleven
of fifteen passing for 211 yards and four touchdowns with no interceptions.
But it was his scrambling and keepers that drove Edelman and the Bay City
coaching staff crazy. Every time it appeared the defense had him for a loss,
the junior QB would scramble out for a huge gain. All of this only served to
open things up for Quizz, who finished the night with 193 yards and three
scores himself. The contest became a scoring frenzy for Lamar.

Bay City, led by strong-armed quarterback Shaun Rutherford, managed a
second-place tie in district that year but lost in the first round of the playoffs
to Texas City. Edelman's Air-raid offense was tailored around Rutherford's
talent and skill set. But Bay City was no longer the dream job for most high
school coaches. Edelman left after only one season to take the head coaching position at Arlington Sam Houston high school. Rutherford, who was
6'0" and 180 pounds and obviously talented, could not carry the team deep
into the playoffs. Bay City's struggles continued as the population continued to shrink, taking talent away from the coastal town. Meanwhile Lamar
had the train back on the tracks, at least temporarily, and they could now
settle into trying to win another district title.

The difference a couple of weeks made was obvious as the Mustangs never
relaxed during their 62-14 trouncing of Bay City. Rodgers saw very little celebrating even with so much offensive output. "Guys were happy and all, but
nobody was running around acting out. It was business all night. You knew
you were being graded every play. I just wanted to get one in the books and
move forward."

Coach Wilson saw progress also and a distinct change in attitude. The
kids were focused and ready for a deep playoff run. DD Goodson, whose

older brother Justin was spelling the injured Osagiede at inside linebacker was impressed with the Mustang varsity. The sophomore wideout spent the night trying to get used to the speed of the game. "I had to play faster and focus on not making any mistakes. Quizz and the other starters were at a whole different level."

One unexpected bright spot was the play of sophomore defensive end D'Vonn Brown. At 6'1" and 225 pounds, Brown showed he had the size and athleticism to contribute right away. With senior defensive end Deante Ester still sidelined with his injured left arm, Brown's efforts were much needed, and he continued to contribute at a high level the rest of the season. Brown was familiar with the varsity but still not sure where he would fit in. "I wanted to play quickly but these were the guys who I looked up to. I simply did not want to make any mistakes and let the team down. But after Bay City I knew I could contribute right away." For Brown, practice had been harder than his first varsity game.

Coach Matthews saw the increased intensity in practice as well. Things were suddenly different. Matthews knew College Park was not indicative of who Lamar was. "I had always been about accountability, discipline, and such. This fit in well with the coaches that were there. Practice was a super competitive environment." Everyday coaches Franklin (defensive line) and Matthews would compete and talk smack to each other. Who was going to win between the O line and the D line?

"Franklin and I would actually get into a heated battle and get mad. The players saw this competitiveness and they fed off of it." Then later during practice, or soon after, they would see Franklin and Matthews cool down and come together as colleagues and friends. The kids learned brotherhood and closeness. Sometimes the kids themselves would get a little too competitive. The coaches started telling kids not to tackle Quizz because he was breaking guys' collarbones running over them. He broke three different players' collarbones. And when he wasn't running over people, he was making crazy moves in tight spaces because he absolutely hated being tackled, even in practice. It was a whole different level of competitiveness.

Linebacker coach Ayro was aware of it too. He often had to settle Osagiede down because of Sule's competitiveness with Quizz. Every practice would have some personal battles and Ayro had to remind them to focus on the opposition. There was a small group that hung out with Quizz. One of his buddies was playing secondary one day in practice and went to make an open field tackle on Quizz. Rodgers blew him up. The coaches were a little surprised. Quizz told him that on the football field "it's all business, no friend stuff. After practice, friends."

After this particular play, Quizz stomped back to the huddle. He saw somebody in his periphery on a stationary bicycle. He turned his head just long enough to catch Sule's scowl, and nod of approval. He purposely walked through the defensive huddle so that all could hear. With his chinstrap unbuckled, he raised his face mask.

Quizz: Y'all need to make a decision... now.

The season was not going to slip away. He was not going down like that. Like College Park. He took his place in the back of the offensive huddle, chinstrap back on, ready to fight for his dream. Becerra looked around at his defense to observe their reaction. This was a side of Quizz they had never seen before. It was time to put up or shut up. Nobody wanted to hear any more excuses.

SEVEN LAKES

The Mustangs traveled the following Thursday to Katy to take on coach Kevin O'Keefe's Seven Lakes Spartans who were in their second year of playing varsity football. The Spartans kept it respectable early, but the Mustangs pulled away for a 35-14 road victory. O'Keefe's Spartans played about as good as could be expected in the first half. Although Seven Lakes only scored once, they had several clock consuming drives, and their defense only gave up one score in the first two quarters to leave things all tied up 7-7 at the half.

The Spartans were coming off their first ever varsity win the previous week in an upset of Rosenberg Foster. O'Keefe was pleased with his team and knew it would have been tough to contain Rodgers for four quarters. His Spartans had performed decently with what they hoped to do in that first half. Now they just needed to put together a complete game. O'Keefe respected Rodgers and knew the senior running back was always going to do some damage. "We did really well in that first half. Then he did his thing, and we have to learn how to play four quarters. Quizz is special. Good luck containing him for a complete game."

Quarterback Smallwood also made his presence felt when, in the third quarter, with the game all knotted up 14-14, he was flushed out of the pocket and broke free for a 63-yard touchdown jaunt. The rout was on. Rodgers increased his season total to 1,323 yards after another big second half. Coach Wilson was pleased with how his guys responded in the second half, but he knew a real challenge was coming up.

Lamar was not going to be able to wait a half to get going the following week. Wilson knew going from a Saturday to a Thursday game would be tough, but once they got their legs under them it was over against Seven Lakes. Now, Terry High School was sitting there ready for some revenge after dropping the last two to Lamar. Wilson was glad to see Quizz and DJ get going, but more importantly, they would get Osagiede back that next week on defense. There was no relaxing the rest of the way, either, as coach Bob Gillis always had El Campo ready for the district finale. But at that point all Lamar was focused on was Terry.

For the first few weeks following the Elkins game, Osagiede's routine had been the same: some pool rehab and working with the trainers at the field house. Several mornings each week Osagiede met school trainer Lance Hale at the swimming pool at Terry High School, as Lamar had no pool. There they strapped a weighted vest onto Osagiede, and the senior linebacker ran in the pool. He kept his knees high, exaggerating a normal running motion to loosen up his tender left knee. The hope was that he avoided the need for surgery, which would certainly end any hope he had of rejoining the team for the season.

Back at the field house, Hale took Osagiede through a series of exercises designed to strengthen his left knee and also his right leg which would allow for any over-compensation. Hale had Osagiede do quad stretches and then one leg balance drills. Osagiede was able to rejoin practice the week before Terry. He needed to get back up to speed. Wilson needed all hands on deck for the fierce rivalry game against the Rangers.

RIVALRY, B.F. TERRY

Going into the 2007 season Lamar held a 9-8 advantage over the B.F. Terry Rangers in District 24-4A. At the present, Terry was coming off of a 45-14 victory over Foster High School. This contest against Lamar on Saturday night was not just for a district title. These kids all grew up together, played kid league sports together and against each other. The schools shared a stadium. The families went to the same churches and shopped at the same grocery stores. Nobody wanted to go a whole year listening to the other side brag.

DJ Smallwood loved the rivalry game. He knew most of the Terry players. Anthony Brown was one of the best athletes he had ever seen. Of course, there was a lot of trash talking, back and forth, during the game. It was, after all, the "Battle of the Berg." Coach Wilson also was familiar with the importance of this particular game. Lamar had beat Terry the previous two years, so the Rangers were going to be more than ready. Lamar had put it on them in 2006. That kind of stuff got people fired up.

Although the rivalry overall was even, it was more of a series of streaks than back-and-forth. The first meeting was in 1984 and the Mustangs won the first three as Terry was just starting as a program. The Rangers got their first win in 1987 and then there was a break where the teams did not meet for two seasons. When the series resumed in 1990, Lamar again went on a streak of four in a row. The teams then once again went on a break, this time not playing for four years from 1994 to 1997.

When the series resumed in 1998, the Rangers bested Lamar for seven straight years as Lamar's program had fallen into disarray. With the arrival of Wilson and the Rodgers brothers the tide turned, and Lamar pulled out a narrow 28-26 win in 2005. In 2006, with the Big Blue machine humming along in top form, the Rangers were trounced 39-0. It was this loss, and the need to salvage their season, that had Terry pumped up on Saturday night to exact a little revenge.

Terry head coach Tim Teykl was very familiar with Lamar Consolidated, and Jacquizz Rodgers in particular. The Rangers' head man watched both Quizz and James come of age in Richmond as well as their uncle Michael Lewis. He coached their brother Michael Maxwell. All were good athletes. Teykl felt he knew Quizz better than most because his son was the same age. He saw Quizz well before he became known in high school. Kids who grew up in Richmond played pee wee football for the Lamar Hornets or the Rosenberg Roughnecks. Then they would enter school sports and compete against each other in rival middle schools. Teykl remembers it was not just football. "These kids were multi-sport kids, so it was constant competition… football, basketball, track and field."

If there was one complaint from Teykl it was the simple bad luck of how the zoning was drawn up. It could have been his Rangers who were benefiting from all of that talent. Regardless, whenever these two teams met there always was going to be a fight to the finish. Coach Wilson noted that Terry had moved their athletic defensive back/wide receiver, Anthony Brown, into the backfield some the previous week. Wilson knew full-well that everything was on the table in this rivalry. Wilson had grown up in Richmond-Rosenberg. He knew what it was like to lose this particular game. One did not have to be a coaching genius to realize Anthony Brown was a big-play guy and Terry would get the ball in his hands as much as possible.

While many in the district felt it would be another Lamar-El Campo district finale for all of the marbles, Wilson was not going to let his team have another trap game. Most of the teams in district were technically still in it, including Bay City and El Campo. Wilson knew folks wanted to talk about that final game when Lamar went to El Campo. But Terry was going to want to have a say in all of that. On this night he reminded his guys that their entire focus was on Terry and nobody else!

The game lived up to its billing and more. Both teams had dropped down in the state-wide rankings due to early season losses. Both dearly needed this win, not just for district implications, but also because it was that time of year when teams needed to be surging. The Mustangs were the designated home team in the shared stadium and received the opening kickoff. Operating from the power I formation, the Mustangs got Rodgers started quickly. He carried a pitch on first down out to the Lamar 40-yard line. Wilson continued to feed his star running back early, and the Mustangs soon crossed midfield. However, on first down at the Terry 35-yard line Smallwood threw an ill-advised pass and Brown had his first interception of the game.

Terry's All-State, all-everything Anthony Brown played both ways for this game, and remained effective anytime he had the ball in his hands. The Mustang defense knew Brown was going to play his best game of the year. At one point early in the first quarter, defensive coordinator Wade decided it was time to see where his main guy was in his rehab. Osagiede was needed to slow down Brown and the Ranger offense. The defensive leader rode a stationary bike on the sideline in between defensive sets to keep things loose.

The fans clapped as Sule retook his exalted position at inside linebacker, and his teammates suddenly felt a weight lifted off of their shoulders. And another strange feeling. What was it? Could that be hope... a sense of resolve returning to their young souls? As he watched his friend trot onto the field, Quizz whispered a short prayer under his breath.

Please Lord, let my brother shine. If anybody out here deserves it, it's Suk.

On Terry's first possession, Brown took a pitch from quarterback Zach Novak and was quickly into space racing down the Terry sideline before being stopped at the Lamar 34-yard line. Brown used his size and power to break several tackles before hitting the jets for the big gain. It was an omen of things to come. However, this early drive ended just as quickly as it started when a Ranger fumble was recovered by Lamar at their own 24-yard line. And then it was Quizz time. Rodgers took a tite toss at his own thirty and ran first through, and then away from, the entire Ranger defense for the games first score. Taylor Turner's point after was good, and with 7:16 remaining in the first stanza, Lamar had struck first blood.

Brown answered by bringing the ensuing kickoff out to the Terry 40-yard line. The Rangers were unable to get anything going and punted after three and out. The Mustang offense took over at their own twenty. On third and ten, Smallwood found Travis Riedel wide open at the Terry forty for a huge completion. Riedel managed to advance the ball down to the twenty. Quizz finished off the drive with a rugged 12-yard TD run that put Lamar up by two scores with 1:28 left in the quarter. It was not the start Teykl and the Rangers had hoped for. On the Ranger sideline, Brown could only grit his teeth and seethe. This was his opportunity to show his stuff before all of Richmond-Rosenburg as the Rangers were unlikely to advance to the play-offs. The words spilled out of his mouth such that all around him could hear, as he intended. Fortunately, every other Ranger felt exactly the same: Nothing would be sweeter than putting these Mustangs in their place.

Wilson elected to have Turner kick high and short (pooch kick) on the ensuing kickoff rather than kick deep to Brown. Still, the Rangers managed to get the ball back to their own 44-yard line. Teykl continued to put the ball in Brown's hands and his star responded. Breaking tackles and knifing through a swarming Mustang defense, Brown steadily moved the chains. With the Mustang defense keying on Brown, quarterback Ray Cervenka was able to slip out of the backfield and hit his receiver in the end zone for Terry's first score of the night. Terry had answered and nobody on either side was surprised.

The Lamar offense struggled in its next series, but a fake punt run by Carlos Becerra netted a first down at midfield. Quizz then took a screen pass to the Terry 38-yard line where the Ranger defense stiffened. The ball went over on downs and the Terry faithful came alive in the stands. The momentum stalled just as quickly as Terry was unable to move the ball. Then Lamar blocked the punt, giving the Mustangs a first down at the Ranger twenty-seven. It was a prime opportunity for Lamar to retake control of the contest.

After several hard runs by Quizz, the Mustangs found themselves with first and goal at the eight. With less than a minute on the clock the Mustangs went into their hurry-up offense. But the clock expired with the ball at the one-foot line. Terry had averted disaster. A two-score lead in this game would have been huge with the way the defenses and turnovers had dictated things.

Terry started the third quarter with excellent field position at their own 44-yard line. The Mustangs stacked the box against Brown, but he continued to gobble up yardage. Pounding his fullback inside and getting Brown into space on the outside, Teykl saw his offense methodically drive down the field. Brown took it in for another score from the Lamar eight. With the PAT good the Rangers suddenly found themselves in the lead with 6:21 remaining in the third quarter. Defensive coordinator Lane Wade and his Mustangs were going to have to come up with an answer for Anthony Brown.

The Lamar offense responded with a heavy dose of Rodgers, who escaped on third and two for a thirty-yard scamper down to the Terry 33-yard line. On second down Smallwood hit a wide-open Riedel in the end zone but the ball bounced off of his hands for an incompletion. The drive stalled out at the Terry 10-yard line when the Mustangs failed on a fourth and two. It was another promising drive that the Mustangs failed to capitalize on. Teykl went right back to the hot hand of Anthony Brown who continued to gash the interior of the Lamar defense for good yardage. The third quarter ended with the Rangers at their own 41-yard line and chewing up both clock and yardage.

Brown became a man possessed. He pounded through numerous arm tackles on three consecutive runs down to the Lamar 26-yard line. At that point, the Mustangs defense found its resolve and put Terry into a fourth and three. Terry set up in field goal formation, but Lamar's Chuck Obi sniffed out the fake and yelled at the defense to watch out. Obi had guessed correctly, and Terry went back into offensive formation. Then Teykl called a timeout and sent his kicker back out, electing to get some points in this defensive standoff. It was all a part of the chess match between Wilson and Teykl. The field goal attempt was no good.

THE CATCH PART I

On first down, Quizz took a pitch and was off for a big gain, being driven out at the 50-yard line. At one point Rodgers reached the Terry 20-yard line, but then mistakes, penalties, and fumbles left the Mustangs with fourth and long at the Ranger 43-yard line. From the shotgun Smallwood sent Quizz in motion out of the backfield. He took the snap and was immediately hit with a heavy Terry pass rush. Sidestepping several would-be tacklers, Smallwood was able to launch a bomb down to the 5-yard line where a Terry defensive back was in perfect position for the interception. At the last second, Obi came from behind the defender and snatched the ball out of the air for a miraculous completion. It was the athleticism and field awareness that allowed Obi to turn a sure game-ending interception into what became known in Richmond-Rosenberg as "the catch." Rodgers took the handoff on first down and plowed into the end zone to put the Mustangs up 19-14 with only 2:06 left in the game.

Wilson elected to go for two points. It seemed to be an easy decision in the moment. An extra point really accomplished nothing, while a two-point conversion would put Lamar up by a touchdown. And the play call was in Wilson's favor because everybody in the stadium knew Quizz was virtually unstoppable from a few yards outside the goal line. Which is why Wilson called play action. As he guessed, the Terry defense stacked the line of scrimmage. Smallwood faked the handoff to Rodgers and rolled out to his right. If the pass wasn't there he had the size and strength to power into the end zone. However, he spotted Becerra flaring out to the right corner of the end zone. The attempted pass went over the head of Becerra into the waiting hands of Anthony Brown in the back of the end zone. Brown broke two quick tackles and hit the Terry sideline. Even after playing the entire game on offense and defense, Brown had enough speed to easily run away from the Mustangs for two points for Terry and put them in sight of a tie. The Rangers now needed only a field goal to keep this night going.

The Terry sideline and their fans erupted after the sudden turn of events. Now it was up to their offense to keep their hopes alive. Wilson elected again not to kick to Brown deep and had Turner squib-kick down the middle. The only problem was, though, that the Terry players let the ball go between them and it bounced down to the Terry 17-yard line into the waiting arms of Anthony Brown. The senior scooped up the ball and juked several defenders at midfield. He then cut towards the Terry sideline and accelerated. He was finally shoved out of bounds at the Lamar nineteen. The craziness for Wilson and the Mustangs seemed to jump out of every possible situation. What was it? Were the stars misaligned?

On first down Brown carried down to the Lamar 14-yard line. Now there was less than a minute remaining in the contest. Terry had time for only two or three more plays. A handoff to the fullback took the ball to the ten where linebacker Cory Green made the stop. A keeper by quarterback Cervenka gave the Rangers a first and goal, but only seconds on the clock. Teykl gave his star one more shot, and Brown went all the way to the 1-inch line. At this point, with no more time-outs, and having a solid kicker in Paul Rosales, the Terry coach elected to kick it and take his chances in overtime. Rosales split the uprights with only five seconds remaining in the contest and things were all knotted up 19-19.

The night could not have been any stranger, and here they were back where they started. Wilson knew his guys had not looked past this game and yet they still could not put away the resilient Rangers. Finding themselves in overtime was not surprising for the Mustangs. Terry was playing at a level they always did when facing Lamar. The Mustangs were ready for this kind of game and the players and coaches knew the significance of losing. The intensity level on the Mustang sideline was palpably growing. It was far too late in the season for Lamar to be making these same mental mistakes. How in the world could they ever expect to make a deep run in the playoffs while playing at this level mentally? On the sideline, Wilson said very few words. The "look" said it all. Wilson wasn't a screamer. He didn't jump up and down and rant and rave. His voice was calm, his instructions precise. But that look… that look was deafening. His calm demeanor may have belied the fire raging inside, but he would never allow those emotions to escape. His consistent collectedness revealed his expectations in a crystal-clear fashion: Make it happen, get it done, finish this now.

Terry got the first possession in overtime and drove early. But the Mustang defense stiffened. Facing a fourth down, Teykl decided to kick a field goal, which was successful. Down 22-19, the Mustang offense sensed the time had come to put this one in the books. They drove down to the Terry 10-yard line for a first and goal. Smallwood took the snap and pump-faked to tight end Dominique Briggs in the middle of the end zone. He then faked a run, drawing in the Terry defense, which freed up Mustang receiver Travis Riedel for a touchdown toss. Smallwood dropped the pass in just behind

Brown who was covering Riedel. It was perfection in motion. Smallwood had alerted Riedel before the play to be ready. "Probably one of DJ's better throws I would say" recalls Riedel. "Cause one foot short and AB would have picked it."

The Mustangs erupted into a celebration after a hard fought 25-22 overtime win. Cory Green was relieved after the roller coaster victory. "It was everything from Chuck's big catch to the crazy extra point attempt returned the other way. It did not matter who was or wasn't on the field, it was always competitive with those guys. I had gone to middle school with Anthony Brown and even then he was a stud." On this night, Green and the Lamar defense never really stopped him.

Coach Teykl was proud of his guys. "Helluva game, largest crowd ever at Traylor. Packed house. We had them beat in regulation and then Quizz found the end zone to put us down with almost no time left. The single finest game performance by an individual that night was not displayed by Jacquizz Rodgers but by his good friend Anthony Brown, who ended the night with 381 all-purpose yards." For the night, Quizz had close to 300 all-purpose yards himself. The two star players combined for nearly 700 yards of offensive production.

Rodgers also grew up with Brown and the two were friends. Rodgers felt relieved as he left the field that night. "He [Brown] was their best player and had a heckuva game. We barely won. That game seemed to get us fired up mentally and emotionally. We were ready to finish up against El Campo and felt healthy going into the end of the season, finally."

Terry's Brown had to take consolation in the fact that he left it all out on the field. Being friends with Quizz since fifth grade brought out the competitiveness in both of them. Brown knew going into the game they both would have to bring it every play. Now, with his season winding down, all Brown could do was hope for the best for his childhood buddy. Terry was most likely done for the season, and Anthony Brown had given the Rangers everything he had on this night, and every other night. Brown was selected to the Class 4-A All-state team as a defensive back.

FOSTER

John and Randolph Foster High School was built in 2001 in unincorporated Fort Bend County. The school was situated north of Rosenberg which was home to both B.F. Terry High and Lamar Consolidated. Prior to the building of Foster, the town had its own cross-town rivalry know around those parts as the "Battle of the Berg" in reference to Richmond-Rosenberg.

But on this Friday night Foster was not interested in hearing anything about that rivalry. They felt like the new kid on the block who had to prove he belonged. This was going to be a three-team town and they had every intention of being a tough out at the least. The Mustangs received the opening kickoff and immediately went to the flea flicker pass play. The exchange between Rodgers and Smallwood was fumbled, and the Mustangs were instantly in a hole. The next two plays went nowhere, and the Foster defense had forced a three and out. The punt was returned to midfield and the Falcon faithful, who were designated the home team in the shared stadium, were fired up early.

The excitement did not last long as the swarming Mustang defense got their own three and out to kill Foster's early momentum. Behind the passing of Smallwood and the running of Rodgers the offense started clicking. But a lost fumble at the Falcon's 30-yard line killed the promising drive. With Osagiede now back into the mix, the Lamar defense remained stubborn. Defensive coordinator Wade had Sule line up close to the line of scrimmage to blitz in what he called a "Will Squeeze." Sule's extraordinary quickness got him into the backfield so fast that a handoff could barely be made. Foster had to punt again, and this time Rodgers showed his return skills by taking the ball back to the Foster 39-yard line. A Smallwood pass to sophomore receiver Jamal Williams took the ball to the Foster 24-yard line.

Foster started loading the box and blitzing to take away the power game of Lamar. Wilson countered by going to his passing game, but the series ended on downs and Foster took over at its own 24-yard line. The first quarter ended scoreless with the two defenses dominating a sloppy game by both offenses. Lamar's ineffectiveness early in recent games did not go unnoticed by the coaching staff. Coach Matthews knew he needed his guys to learn to get out of the gate quicker. "Slow starts are due to lack of focus, defensive game plans by the opposition, personnel changes, and so on. Play calling is a rhythmic thing… it's a feeling… and you have to get into a groove and that sometimes doesn't happen right away. Still, that needed to change with the playoffs looming large."

The Falcon offense continued its futility and Lamar soon had the ball back at their own 34-yard line. Foster, with eight men in the box, continued to control the vaunted Mustang rushing attack. Wilson put the game in his junior quarterback's hands. Smallwood hit Obi at the forty where he broke a tackle and carried the ball to midfield. From the shotgun with a one-back set, Smallwood pump faked and gave the ball to Rodgers on a delayed hand-off. Quizz quickly hit the outside running left and was off to the races. He was finally taken down at the Foster twelve. Three more Rodgers runs, and Lamar was on the board first. Taylor Turner's point after was good and, with 7:11 remaining in the second quarter, the Lamar offense had found a good mix of run and pass.

On Foster's next drive their offense also started finding some success through the air. After a huge completion on second down to their own 45-yard line, they followed up with a big run by Issac Kerr to the Lamar forty-three. Suddenly things were looking up for the Falcons. But then the drive stalled out at the thirty when a fumbled snap and a quarterback sack took Foster out of field goal range. A touchback set up the Mustang offense with first down at their twenty.

The series started terribly, and Lamar was looking at a third and fifteen when Smallwood took the snap from the shotgun and, from his own 5-yard line, launched a rocket to the Falcon forty where he connected with a wide-open Travis Riedel. The senior wideout hauled it in and rambled down to the Foster twenty-five. The crowding of the line of scrimmage by Foster had come back to bite them again.

With time running out in the second quarter Wilson decided to open up his offense. Two more Smallwood passes set up the Mustangs with first and goal at the four. Smallwood then used his legs to scramble out of trouble and took it in for Lamar's second score of the night. Turner's point after was good and, with just two seconds remaining in the half, Lamar had opened up a two-score lead.

Foster received the second half kick and set up at their twenty. Osagiede could not help but scowl at the Falcon sign above the entrance to the locker rooms. Because Traylor Stadium was on the campus of Lamar, the sign in front of the locker room entrance had Mustang Football painted on it. When either Terry or Foster were designated as the home team against Lamar, these teams placed temporary signs over the Mustang one. Although it was a fair thing to do, it tended to get under the skin of some of the more spirited Lamar players. And nobody was more spirited than Sule. With Osagiede and Obi crowding the line of scrimmage the Falcons went back to the air. However, on second down, QB Young's pass was picked off by corner Andrew Okokhere at the Falcon thirty-two and returned to the 1-yard line. Then Okokhere had the ball knocked out of his hands. The Falcons recovered on their own 1-yard line to avert disaster.

Foster's Isaac Kerr carried them out of this hole to the Lamar 20-yard line where things got heated. A dead ball foul resulted in fifteen more yards for the Falcons. Near the action, linebacker Chuck Obi raised his hands and pleaded his case with the line judge. But the man in zebra stripes had already made up his mind. It was what is referred to in football jargon as a "ticky-tack" foul, but resulted in the ejection of Obi, and fired up the Falcon sideline. The players had gotten chatty, and the referees were not about to let this one get out of hand. Suddenly the Foster offense found its stride, and the pushing and jawing continued after almost every play. Foster had no intention of being intimidated. Quarterback Young was running the option to perfection against a Mustang defense that had seemingly lost its focus.

Another big run by Kerr had the Falcons with first and ten at the Lamar five. However, on the next play, the ball was stripped by linebacker Cory Green and the Mustangs recovered. A quick pass on first down to sophomore Jamal Williams got the Mustangs some breathing room at their own twenty. The drive then seemed to be stalling out after the Mustangs went backwards. But on third and twenty, Smallwood hit Quizz on a screen pass at the Mustang 18-yard line. Rodgers broke through two tackles and turned up the left sideline. There he encountered two more Falcon defenders. He broke these two tackles and reversed field, heading across the fifty towards the right sideline. He then broke a fifth tackle and ran down the middle of the field into the end zone for his third score of the night. It was typical Jacquizz Rodgers, using his excellent open field vision and his blockers every step of the way.

Coach Matthews' rule of never giving up on a Rodgers' run had paid dividends yet again. The score effectively took the fight out of the upstart Falcons. Turner's PAT was good, and Lamar had a commanding three score lead. What's more, the brief surge in momentum the Falcons had mustered following the big personal foul penalty had quickly wilted. The hallmark quick strike capability of the Mustangs continued to be a common theme in the remainder of the 2007 season.

The Mustang defensive pressure on Falcon quarterback Young ended any hopes the Falcons had of getting something going offensively. Another heavy dose of Rodgers had the Mustangs with a first down at the Foster twenty-five. Quizz then took a pitch from Smallwood and cut thru the middle of the line. He made a sudden move to his right and outran everybody to the right corner of the end zone for his fourth score of the night. Turner connected on another point after and with just 3:05 left in the contest the Falcons were all but done.

The Foster offense still had its pride, though, and they ended the game with an impressive drive for their only score of the night with just five seconds left on the game clock. It was the kind of statement of character that would serve Foster High School well on the football field for years to come. But this night belonged to the surging Mustangs.

EL CAMPO

The following week the Ricebirds from El Campo traveled to Traylor Stadium expecting to have another of their historical battles with Lamar Consolidated. What they encountered was a team that felt it was hitting its stride at just the right time. Wilson felt good about his team after they outlasted Terry and brushed off Foster. "Last game of district play, and we were starting to play at a different level. Offense was clicking on the ground and in the air. Defense was back healthy and starting to play at a high level." Coach Wilson always said that people thought that Lamar won because of what they did offensively, but it was their defense that put them over the top.

The Ricebirds received the opening kickoff which junior Adan Gomez boomed out of the end zone for a touchback. Coach Gillis had put his offense on the backs of quarterback Dakota Pietsch and running back Anthony Terrell. However, Pietsch broke his collar bone and did not return until the playoffs. In his place Tyler Woods tried to keep the big red machine in the playoff hunt. Quarterback was not Woods' normal position.

On the first series, Woods rolled right and tried to hit his receiver in the flat. Rover Chuck Obi jumped the route at the last second and intercepted the ball at the El Campo 19-yard line. The Mustang offense came out flat and settled for an attempted field goal of 37-yards. Taylor Turner's attempt was blocked, and the Ricebirds returned it all the way for a touchdown. At the 9:38 mark of the first quarter, El Campo was on the board thanks to its special teams play. Wilson could only shake his head. When were these Mustangs ever going to learn that a team can never relax?

The Ricebirds elected to pooch kick in order to keep the ball out of Rodgers' hands, giving Lamar excellent starting position at their own 41-yard line. A steady diet of Rodgers kept the chains moving. On first and goal from the eight, the Mustangs used misdirection and the pulling of guard Presley Godson to get Quizz out into the left flat and in for his first score of the night. Turner's point after was good and with 7:32 remaining in the opening quarter the game was all tied.

On El Campo's next offensive series, the defensive front of D'Vonn Brown, Clarence Ward, Colin Usen and Andrew Nwaogwugwu dominated. The Ricebirds punted after a three and out. Quizz took a screen pass from Smallwood and sprinted seventy-eight yards for an apparent touchdown. A block in the back penalty against Lamar negated the quick score. Two quick passes to Chuck Obi moved the ball past midfield. The drive eventually stalled out at the El Campo fifteen. The Mustang offense was suddenly out of sync.

The first quarter came to an end with both offenses having made multiple mistakes. On third down, the Ricebirds' Woods attempted a long pass that was picked off by Lamar's Quentin Palmer at the Mustang 40-yard line. Back on offense, Wilson continued to show the Ricebird defense multiple sets. On second and one, Smallwood connected again with Obi, taking the ball to the El Campo 30-yard line. Then, with a split backfield, Smallwood threw a backwards pass to Quizz, who then fired into the end zone. He hit sophomore wideout DD Goodson in the back of the end zone for Lamar's second score of the night.

Turner's point after was good and with 8:52 left in the half Lamar had its first lead. Occasional trick plays kept defenses from stacking the box against the Mustang offense. Wilson rarely called trick plays, but when he did, they usually worked because he saw something specific that the other team was doing. Plus, it gave opposing coaches something else to think about.

On El Campo's next drive, Gillis realized his passing game was not his best option and went to the run game. His Ricebirds responded with some hard-nosed football. The tactic worked, and, with 3:11 remaining in the second stanza, they scored to tie the ball game.

A chop block on the ensuing kickoff put the Mustangs at their own 3-yard line with time running out on the first half. The drive was saved on third and ten when Smallwood hit Rodgers coming out of the backfield.

Some nifty running by Quizz took the ball out to the Lamar twenty. Then the series turned disastrous. After several penalties, the Mustangs elected to punt on fourth and twenty. Alex Rohdes' snap went over Turner's head and out of the back of the end zone for a safety. With 39 seconds remaining in the half, El Campo was back in the lead. This was not the time of year for the Mustangs to be unfocused. Wilson gathered his team and gave them the look. Nothing had to be said. Lamar prided themselves on being mentally tough. It was a tense locker room at the half.

What should have been a fired-up Mustang locker room scene instead became a lot of teeth gritting as multiple players were admonished by the coaching staff. It didn't take long for the team leaders to take matters into their own hands. Few words were spoken amongst the players, but those words served the purpose. This team had to realize that time was running out for them to put all of the pieces together. The Mustangs received the second half kickoff and set up at their own 40-yard line. On first down, Quizz took the pitch and ran left side. He cut behind a pulling Godson and accelerated into the secondary. Sixty yards later, the Mustangs had reclaimed the lead. The two-point attempt failed and with just twelve seconds off the clock the Mustangs had regained the momentum.

The Mustang defense, with the exhortation of their leader Osagiede, forced a three and out on the Ricebirds' first two possessions. Lamar's offensive woes continued as well, but theirs were due to mental mistakes leading to more penalties. At one point they had a first and thirty-five at their own fifteen. But then Wilson went back to Rodgers on a screen and Quizz answered with an 85-yard touchdown run. It was a backbreaker for the Ricebirds who had been solidly in this game to that point.

Suddenly the kicking team was fired up and the Lamar defense fed off of this exuberance. It had been a long season, filled with injuries and uncertainties. Now these Mustangs were starting to feel it and they were ready to put the finishing touches on another district championship in front of their home crowd. Osagiede was plowing into the middle on every run by El Campo, defying them to try and get past the line of scrimmage. Linebacker Cory Green did likewise. This had become a personal challenge to shut the Ricebirds down completely the rest of the way.

Defensive end Deante Ester, with his left arm heavily wrapped, had come into the game for his first action since early in the season. The senior defense end was ready to get himself back into football shape. On a fourth and one,

Ester knifed through to stop El Campo short, thus ending all hopes the Rice-birds had of reversing the momentum. Then it was up to Quizz to chew up the fourth quarter clock.

Quizz managed to break a second down run to midfield, but another costly penalty put the Mustangs in third and long. Smallwood set four receivers in the formation and hit a wide-open Travis Riedel for a 50-yard touchdown to seal the deal. The Ricebirds actually had a promising drive going midway through the fourth, but on third down Woods was hit by Ward as he was attempting to throw a pass. Free safety Fleming collected the errant throw and returned it ninety-six yards for another Lamar score. The first team all-State free safety played center field better than anybody in the country.

At that point Wilson cleared his bench, allowing some of the reserves to enjoy this final district game. The Ricebirds managed to score with a couple of minutes left in the game. This squad from El Campo had a proud tradition in high school football and they refused to quit. Sophomore Marcel Threat replaced Rodgers in the backfield. Quizz's night included some big runs on screen plays adding another weapon to Wilson's arsenal heading into the playoffs. The Mustangs had hoped to meet La Marque in the first round, but Dickinson had upset the Cougars, setting up a first-round meeting between the Gators and Lamar Consolidated. Dickinson was favored by two touchdowns when the two teams met the following week.

As the final seconds ticked off the clock, the home crowd fans were on their feet. The Mustang regular season had been a roller coaster. Their goals to this point had been to win district and get healthy. This night had not turned out as planned in spite of the huge victory. They had too many mental errors and penalties. For a team that prided itself on discipline this was not how the Mustangs wanted to play with the playoffs up next. There was work to be done on Monday.

Once Wilson saw his team rebound from the early season losses, he knew he had a chance. Certain things would have to happen, such as players finally staying healthy. But the number of pleasant surprises far outweighed the negatives. He had a coaching staff that had come together. and the parts were clicking. He had a team that was showing resolve and character. And he had Jacquizz Rodgers. Richmond-Rosenberg was once again Wilson's town.

1. Jacquizz Rodgers as a Hornet (courtesy Jacquizz Rodgers family photos)
Rodgers knew from an early age that he wanted to be a running back.

2. James, Tasha, Michael, Quizz and Cartai. (courtesy Williams family photos)
Tasha raised her four children as a single mom.

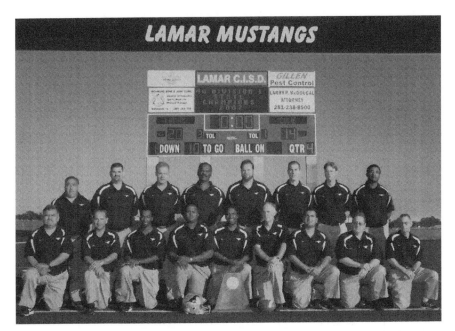

3. 2007 Mustang Coaching Staff. Front row: Hernandez, Peloquin, Humphrey, Matthews, Wilson, Wade, Romero, Fyke, Thompson. Back row: Velazquez, Hale, Hummel, Franklin, Kobza, Callahan, Urinak, Ayro

4. Coach Charlie Ayro and Sule Osagiede. Coach Ayro had his hands full with his inside linebacker and defensive captain Osagiede

STATE FARM/TEXAS FOOTBALL 4A TOP 25			
	'06 Overall	'06 District	Returnees
1. Copperas Cove	12-3	5-1	7/5
2. Stephenville	10-2	6-1	9/5
3. Wolfforth Frenship	12-3	4-0	7/9
4. Waco	13-3	5-0	5/7
5. Wichita Falls Rider	9-5	5-1	7/8
6. La Marque	15-1	6-0	4/3
7. Brownwood	7-7	4-2	7/7
8. Rosenberg Lamar	13-1	5-0	6/6
9. Corpus Christi Calallen	12-1	5-0	6/6
10. Aledo	12-2	6-1	4/5
11. New Braunfels	8-4	5-2	6/4
12. Highland Park	11-1	6-0	2/4
13. Texas High	12-1	5-0	3/2
14. Denton Ryan	7-4	6-1	8/6
15. Friendswood	7-4	4-2	8/5
16. Corpus Christi Flour Bluff	10-3	4-1	5/6
17. Beeville Jones	9-3	5-1	7/7
18. Dayton	9-3	7-0	7/4
19. Brenham	11-2	6-0	6/4
20. New Braunfels Canyon	7-3	4-3	7/3
21. Lake Travis	8-3	7-0	6/6
22. Corsicana	5-6	4-2	5/6
23. Rosenberg Terry	7-4	4-1	5/7
24. Keller Fossil Ridge	10-2	6-0	6/3
25. Gregory-Portland	4-6	2-3	10/5

5. 2007 Preseason Poll. Dave Campbell's Texas Football magazine preseason rankings. The Mustangs began the season ranked eighth in one poll.

6. Head Coach Lydell Wilson. Coach Wilson knew as long as he had Rodgers, Smallwood, Obi and Osagiede, he had a chance to win it all.

7. Offensive Coordinator Pat Matthews. Offensive Coordinator Matthews advised his offensive line to never give up on a Jacquizz Rodgers run.

8. Defensive End Deante Ester. Defensive end Ester returned from an injury to his left arm during the season to lead a swarming defense in the playoffs.

9. Defensive captain Sule Osagiede. Linebacker Osagiede rode a stationary bicycle on the sideline to help keep his tender left knee warm throughout the games.

10. Guy K. Traylor Stadium. Traylor Stadium, located on the campus of Lamar Consolidated High School was a shared stadium for the Mustangs, Terry Rangers, and Foster Falcons.

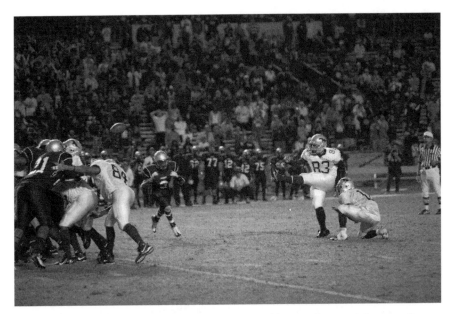

11. Kicker Adan Gomez. Gomez kicked a field goal in overtime to defeat Austin LBJ and send Lamar into another semi-final contest, this time against undefeated New Braunfels.

12. New Braunfels quarterback Ryan Perez. Unicorn QB Ryan Perez kept his team alive through three overtimes in the semi-final contest against Lamar Consolidated.

13. Free Safety Steven Fleming. All-State Free Safety Fleming broke his wrist in the first overtime against New Braunfels. His replacement for the state game was Jacquizz Rodgers.

14. Team trainers Dennis Fyke and Lance Hale. Trainers Fyke and Hale were busier than expected after a rash of early season injuries.

15. Copperas Cove Defensive Coordinator Reb Brock and Linebacker Tanner Brock. Cove DC Brock depended on his son, linebacker Tanner, to lead the Bulldawg defense against the Mustangs.

16. Copperas Cove coaches Tracy and Jack Welch. DC Tracy Welch and his brother, Head Coach Jack Welch had Copperas Cove in the state championship once again in 2007 following a tough loss to Alamo Heights for the title in 2006.

17. Rowdiest Individuals of Texas. Some members of the RIOT group went shirtless in the freezing temperatures at the state game to prove their spirit for the Mustangs.

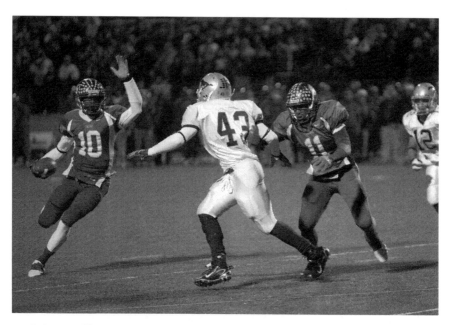

18. Robert Griffin III and Sule Osagiede. Mustang linebacker Sule Osagiede and his defense were tasked with keeping RG III under wraps in the state contest.

19. Jacquizz Rodgers. Quizz knew that it would be a fierce contest anytime he and the Mustangs faced the Terry Rangers in the "Battle of the Berg".

20. Quarterback DJ Smallwood and running back Jacquizz Rodgers. Coach Wilson used his potent one-two punch of QB Smallwood and RB Rodgers to keep Copperas Cove off-balance in the state championship in Round Rock.

SECTION III

CHAPTER 8

PLAYOFF UNDERDOGS

Dickinson Gators

The Mustangs were slotted into Division I of the 2007 Texas Class 4 A playoffs. With another district championship under their belts the Mustangs were ready to make a deep run. They were finally healthy after a season that was plagued with injuries. With Jacquizz Rodgers living up to his billing and the defensive starters all back, coach Wilson liked his team's chances going forward. Wilson felt at that point if he got his opponent to the fourth quarter with a lead or close, Lamar was going to win the game. As a coach, that was the greatest feeling in the world. Confidence was high in the field house at Traylor. The fans and pundits were still skeptical.

The Mustangs found themselves on the right side of the playoff bracket in Region 3 of Division I. The obvious roadblocks were Brenham, Port Neches-Groves, Dickinson, New Braunfels, and defending state champion San Antonio Alamo Heights. However, the more difficult half of the bracket appeared to be the left side. The number one team in the state in 4A, Copperas Cove was slotted to come from that half. However, they were no sure bet. The likes of state powers such as Waxahachie, Aledo, McKinney Boyd, and Marshall were also vying to come from that half of the bracket. First things first though for the Mustangs and that meant escaping a bi-district showdown with the Gators from Dickinson.

After facing the disappointment in not meeting La Marque in the opening round of the championship playoffs, the players quickly turned their focus to the Dickinson Gators. This bi-district contest was going to be a good litmus test of how good these Mustangs could be.

PLAYOFFS DIVISION I CLASS 4 A

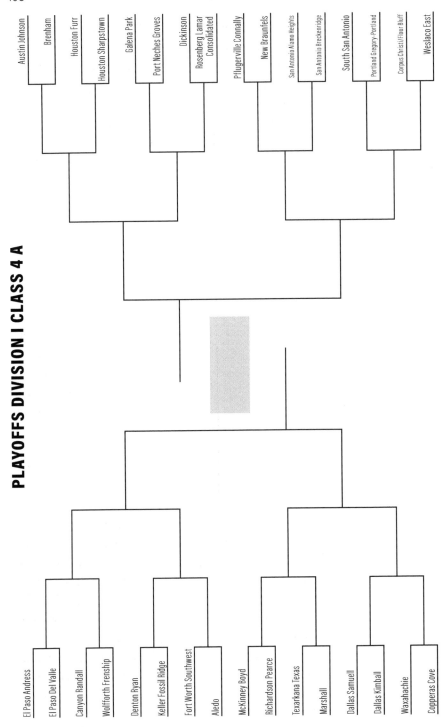

Several defensive starters continued to deal with lingering issues, but nothing was going to keep the seniors off the field. Osagiede was stronger, benefitting tremendously from his off-season workouts and conditioning. Still present was the stationary bicycle on the sideline. Defensive tackle Mason Quintanilla also started feeling stronger and was dealing with less pain from his gunshot wounds. Linebacker Carlos Becerra nursed his ankle sprain throughout the playoffs, but he also benefitted from strenuous off-season workouts. Ester was back, and well-rested, his scarred forearm heavily wrapped each day.

On Thursday afternoon the team gathered for one last walk through. Playing this bi-district contest at home was definitely an advantage, but Wilson did not want his troops relaxing one bit. He kept the tone serious. The offense was reminded that Dickinson had stood toe to toe with some the most potent offenses in the state in their own district. Meanwhile Coach Wade harped on how explosive Colbert Archie could be. And Gator quarterback Clay Honeycutt would be more than ready if the Mustang defense keyed on Archie. There were ample reasons why the media had Dickinson favored. Dickinson was just a few miles down I-45, so this home field advantage wasn't really an advantage at all. The truth remained that navigating a district with Texas City and defending state champion La Marque had the Gators somewhat already battle tested. The Mustangs had stumbled often up to this point in the season.

Looking up into the stands on Wednesday, Osagiede saw few onlookers for the first time all season. There was no doubt that the Lamar faithful were not living vicariously through their high school football team. Oh, they would show up en masse and even arrive early on the following Friday night. After all, they were all friends and family. They either grew up together or possibly even married into each other's families. They came to support their team, but this was also a chance to catch up from their busy lives. Sure, they wanted their kids to win, but their lives did not hinge on it. Osagiede looked back into his defensive huddle. This was his family. These were the people he played for. As he reached down to rub his sore knee, he thought of all the questions to which he was still searching for answers.

On the sideline, Quizz sipped on lukewarm water from the sideline hydrating station. He saw that his Nigerian childhood friend was deep in thought. This brought questions of his own. Would Sule's tender knee hold up? Would this bunch finally put it all together and make another decent run into the playoffs? How would he reconcile anything other than a championship in his own mind? The answer came in that it was time to trust Wilson and the system that had been so carefully put in place. They had done everything possible to prepare for this postseason. Last year was last year. Opportunity to make it all right was now sitting there in front of him.

Dickinson was one of many Gulf Coast programs that had a history of playing excellent football. The 1986 Dickinson Gators had Andre Ware as their signal caller. They were upset in the first round of the state 4A playoffs by eventual champion West Orange Stark. Ware went on to stardom as quarterback for the University of Houston around the time of the dawn of the "run and shoot" offense. He set 26 NCAA records and won the Heisman Trophy while the #14 ranked Cougars finished the season 9–2. Ware became the first Houston Cougar to win the Heisman.

Dickinson was also home to quarterback Donnie Little who led the Gators to the state title in Class 3A in 1977. In that championship game against Brownwood, Little ran for 255 yards, which at that time was a state record. One year later the playoff rushing record was broken by none other than Eric Dickerson who led Sealy to a state title. Little became a standout quarterback for the University of Texas.

In 2007 Dickinson entered the year expected to finish no better than fourth in a very tough district that included the likes of perennial power houses La Marque and Texas City. Long gone were the glory days of Little and Ware at Dickinson, which is a town of approximately 18,000 located about 28 miles southeast of Houston on I 45 going to Galveston. The Gators had dealt with some injuries and setbacks of their own. Head coach Warren Trahan had anticipated an exciting season with his son, Brody, as the starting quarterback. But a midseason injury put Brody on the sideline and tight end Clay Honeycutt was inserted at quarterback. Likewise, starting free safety Archie had filled in as a second running back and effectively solidified the position. It was Archie and Honeycutt who led the Gators to a huge end of season victory over reigning state champion La Marque in district play.

Honeycutt, a 6'3" 195 pounder, Archie, and Kenneth Mullins had helped the team power through a tough 8-2 record that included a grueling 14-17 loss in district to Texas City, and the 43-22 eye-opening win over La Marque. The Gators finished district play with a disappointing 29-14 upset loss to Brazosport, which the media attributed to them looking ahead to their contest against Lamar. Because they had navigated such a tough district the Gators were favored over the Mustangs. A coin flip determined the site of the game. Coach Lydell Wilson's luck held out and the bi-district game was scheduled at Traylor stadium in Rosenberg.

During that time, the energy level at the Lamar Consolidated campus reached a feverish pitch. The school was blessed with not only a super talented football team, but also a state ranked baseball program. That 2007-2008 squad was composed of several guys who had been together since little league, and they had players who were part of a US squad that made it to the Little League World Series final. In the outfield, they had slugger Randal Grichuk who was committed to play at Arizona but ended up being drafted in the first round by Major League Baseball. He became a star outfielder for the Toronto Blue Jays. On the mound was ace Brady Rodgers who played collegiately at Arizona State and ended up on the Houston Astros rotation. Joining Grichuk in the outfield were all-district performers Cody Robinson and Cody Abraham who were also college-bound on baseball scholarships.

Brady Rodgers felt the excitement growing day by day as the Mustang football team prepared to take on Dickinson. "The baseball team went to every football game in an attempt to make them all feel like home games. The students called themselves The Rowdiest Individuals of Texas and made RIOT t-shirts to wear to the games. We were all friends in Lamar sports, so the other sports teams wanted that state championship just as much. The RIOT bunch got loud and stayed loud throughout the playoff run."

Ryan Cicatello, a senior at Lamar at the time, enjoyed the excitement around campus. Cicatello joined in with Ryan Haas who started the RIOT group. Said Cicatello: "It was a fun time to be at Lamar Consolidated. For the students it was all about who was carpooling with who, and what signs needed to be made. We had a social media group to organize the road trips. We showed up early to get up front and make some noise."

As the Mustangs went through their last walk throughs on the Thursday preceding the game against Dickinson, Coach Wilson decided it was time for one of his teaching moments. He generally brought these out during special teams practice. There are three phases to a football game: offense, defense, and special teams. While offense and defense tend to garner the lion's share of preparation, good coaches know that it is often something that happens on special teams play that can change the course of a game.

Whether it be a miscue or a quick score, special teams play tends to get less focus by the players.

For that reason, Wilson would often use special teams practice to get his players' attention. He called out the punt team but told the punt receiving team to stay on the sideline with the other coaches. Then he looked around for a victim. Offensive tackle Paul Alford was the lucky one on this day. Wilson wanted to take somebody out of their comfort zone, somebody who would not normally handle a punt, and have that player drop back to receive. As he walked to the sideline, he kept the football tucked in his arm. This gave the team time to respond to this challenge. Here they had one of their guys, Alford, put in a tense situation. The deal was, if Alford caught Taylor Turner's punt, then practice was over, and no sprints would be run. If he mishandled the punt, then they all would line up at the 50-yard line for a sprint. This would be repeated until Alford handled the punt.

The moment was not just about whether they would run sprints or not. Wilson kept the ball from Turner so the team could respond. Suddenly, it was Osagiede who exhorted Alford on. "Come on, Paul, you got this. Look it in all the way." Then next would be Pena, or Obi, or Becerra. "You da man, Paul. Walk in the park." Soon the whole team was yelling and clapping, and the vibe reached a feverish pitch. This was what Wilson was looking for… team unity and spirit. One for all, and all for one. And he needed to see that focus, that little extra something that gives a team an edge. He needed everybody to get their mind on the task at hand.

Wilson pitched the ball to Alex Rohde and the unit went into punt formation. Quiz instructed Alford to back up ten more yards as he was too close. Alford's expression showed he understood the brevity of this moment, but it also belied the fact that he was not amused at being chosen. Turner handled the snap and launched the punt. Alford started back pedaling but quickly realized he was back too far. He started forward slowly but realized he was not going to get there quickly enough. He could not let this ball touch the ground. He timed it perfectly and cradled the ball in his arms like it was his first born. The coaches smiled, the team erupted, and Alford started breathing again. Now, now they were ready to play this game. Tomorrow night was the start of yet another season. Only now every game was single elimination.

The home team Mustangs were in their blue Nike tops and silver pants. The Gators were in their road whites with blue numbers. The opening quarter was uneventful as both defenses dominated and both offenses were plagued by penalties. The feeling out process went into the second quarter. The first score of the half was a Rodgers' touchdown that came after Deante Ester's block of a Yousef Nacouzi punt at the Gator 37-yard line. Several Rodgers' runs put the ball at the Dickinson three. A tite toss from Smallwood to Rodgers seemed to be stopped at the line, but Quizz hit the brakes and accelerated to his right to outrun everyone to the end zone marker. Taylor Turner's PAT was good, and Lamar had struck first with 9:27 remaining in the first half. Next, Mustang quarterback DJ Smallwood found a wide-open Chuck Obi on a 26-yard scoring pass to open up a 13-0 lead. Suddenly, with 4:17 remaining in the half the Lamar offense was clicking on all cylinders.

Meanwhile, the Lamar defensive front four continued to harass Honeycutt on every snap leading to overthrows and near interceptions. With time running out, the Mustangs regained possession with one more shot to score before the half. As Dickinson continued to key on Rodgers, Smallwood used his arm and his legs to keep the chains moving. This opened up things for Quizz who bounced a run outside and took it to the Dickinson 17-yard line with time about to expire. The Mustangs went into their hurry up offense, and with just fourteen seconds left in the half, Quizz scored again making it 19-0. The try for two was no good and the half ended with Lamar leaving the field to loud approval from their hometown fans. The Dickinson faithful were eerily quiet, not sure what to make of these Mustangs.

Lamar received the second half kickoff, hoping to keep the pressure on the Gators. The Dickinson defense came out with a renewed purpose. They knew they needed to figure out this Mustang offense now before things got worse. Once again keying on Quizz, they were able to squelch the run. Then they were able to pressure Smallwood in the pocket to force Lamar into a three and out. Turner's punt got past the return man and rolled to the Gator 10-yard line.

It was time for Dickinson to make some noise on offense. Having averaged almost thirty points per game, the Gator offense had capable weapons. On first down, running back Archie got loose for a 66-yard run that got the Dickinson crowd on their feet. But, just as quickly, Honeycutt threw a pass that was intercepted by Lamar's Quentin Palmer at the Mustang three to kill the potential scoring drive. The turnover was deflating for Dickinson's confidence. On the visitor's sideline, an exasperated Coach Trahan could only shake his head. "We had no problem moving the ball but fell flat on our faces in the red zone."

The Mustangs barely escaped the shadow of their own goal line before they had to punt. However, on the ensuing punt the ball was fumbled at midfield and Lamar's Mason Quintanilla quickly pounced on it for another costly turnover. Nothing was going the Gators' way. Another burst by Quizz and the Mustangs had first and ten at the Gator thirty. This was followed by another big run to the 12-yard line. On third down Rodgers juked and weaved his way in for another score. Turner booted the point after, and the Mustangs were in total control with 4:29 left in the third stanza.

After stalling out at their own forty-four, the boys in white were forced to punt again, and the flood gates opened. Quizz fielded the punt at his own 25-yard line running full speed. He quickly ran past the Dickinson gunners and then split the rest of the team for a coffin-nailing 75-yard touchdown run. In a flash, the third quarter had turned disastrous for the visiting Gators. Taylor's PAT split the uprights and the rout was on with the score at 33-0. Trahan had warned his bunch about just this very situation. "I absolutely told my punter to not let Quizz touch the ball… to put it out of bounds. As soon as I saw Rodgers field it, I knew it was six the other way. That was the straw that broke the camel's back."

Wilson managed to clear his bench by the end of the game. Dickinson stayed in the fight and hung two scores on the Mustangs. Lamar got a late field goal to make the final score 39-14. It appeared that the Mustangs were healthy and ready to make another deep run into the playoffs. For the night, Rodgers accounted for 316 all-purpose yards and five touchdowns. He went over the 2,000-yard rushing mark for the third consecutive season. The five touchdowns put him closer to the Texas state record of 128 held by Cuero's Robert Strait.

If the Gators were surprised by Rodgers' dogged determination to destroy them, Mustang OC Pat Matthews was not. Matthews heard the news before the game that the Touchdown Club of Houston failed to name Quizz as one of their eight finalists for Houston Area Offensive Player of the Year. It was an unforgivable oversight. The word in the locker room was that Quizz was not appreciative of the snub. Rodgers had his typical response, which was to tighten his chin strap a little tighter and go out and prove for the hundredth time that he would come away victorious, even if it meant putting the team on his back to do it. Later in the season when the snub was brought to the attention of New Braunfels' head coach Chuck Caniford, he replied, "If there are eight players in the Houston area better than Rodgers, I'm glad we didn't have to play those teams."

Trahan was also aware of the snub as he was a voting member of the Touchdown Club. "I completely disagreed with the selection. We kept watching film, and I kept telling anybody who would listen that, in Rodgers, we were looking at the best football player in the Houston area, if not the state, and it was not even close. We went into the game knowing exactly what we were up against with Quizz. The problem was we still could not stop him. And their quarterback was very underrated. You had to make a choice on who you were going to stop. Smallwood made us pay all night and then Rodgers did his thing. At the end of the night, I realized they had way more talent on the field than most people realized. We followed them the rest of the way in the playoffs. I knew they were going to give people fits because they were not just talented... one could easily see that those young men were on a mission. They were ready to get down in the trenches and get dirty. And they had the best running back in the country."

For their part, the Mustang defense stymied a Gator offense that was averaging over 330 yards per game. Gator running back Archie did manage to rack up 188 yards on twenty-one carries, but his efforts did not translate into points. The Lamar defense was healthy, and they showed they could be a force now in the playoffs. After the way Dickinson had scored so easily against defending state champion La Marque, many pundits thought they would do the same against a suspect Mustang defense. That was one of the reasons the Gators came in favored. Matthews saw a change in the attitude from the newspapers after this game. "All week they had kind of been talking up Dickinson and sort of making us look like the lesser team. After this game, the media started talking us more seriously."

While the Mustang offense may have seemed to be the story of the night, Lamar Consolidated head coach Wilson was equally impressed with his defense which held the Gators scoreless for most of the contest. "The defense came out and played outstanding. We threw some different looks at them. We kept them off balance and took them out of their game plan. It was good to see our guys reaching their potential finally."

One Mustang who was thrilled to see action again was defensive end Ester. He had missed all of district play except the end of the El Campo game, and he was finally cleared to start for this playoff opener. "I was nervous and excited at the same time. I felt like I had something to prove after being out so long." With the win in the books, the Mustangs now had to wait for the winner of Port Neches-Groves and Galena Park. When it was announced that the PN-G Indians had won 33-0 the Mustangs knew they were headed for a tough regional showdown. The sight was set at Stallworth Stadium in Baytown.

CHAPTER 9

THE NECHES

Port Neches-Groves Indians

The Neches River is one of five major rivers in Texas. It starts in Van Zandt County in east Texas and runs down to Sabine Lake near the Texas-Louisiana border. It runs near several towns and cities including Tyler, Silsbee, Beaumont, and Nederland. Near its end it runs by the neighboring towns of Port Neches and Groves. In 1925, a high school was built in Port Neches to serve portions of Port Neches, Groves, and Port Arthur. The area had a well-known history relating to Native Americans and so the school adopted the nickname Indians. The football team emerged as one of the strongest programs in the state with six appearances in the title game, winning three of those.

In 2007 the PN-G Indians were once again in the playoff mix in Class 4A. However, their season was anything but easy. The Indians started the year by dropping their opener with defending state champion La Marque 19-0. They followed this loss with another scoreless game, falling to Crosby 7-0. Things seemed to turn around from there as they won their next seven games before running into trouble again against an upstart Dayton squad who clobbered the Indians 40-7 in a huge district loss. They rebounded the following week with a strong opening round playoff win over Galena Park, beating the Yellowjackets 33-0. That win propelled them into the regional round against Lamar Consolidated. Lamar had done its part, dispatching a favored Dickinson Gator team 39-14.

It was a chilly and damp Gulf Coast evening in Baytown when the two teams took the field. Lamar head coach Lydell Wilson immediately knew where this game was headed. Lamar was a run first, physical type of football team, so Wilson was okay with the situation even if that was not actually their game plan. Lamar actually went in wanting to throw the football because they felt the Indians could not match up with the Mustang receivers' speed. But the weather changed all of that. The Mustangs were in their blue jerseys with silver pants and silver helmets as the designated home team. The Indians were in their road whites with Purple numbers and their Purple helmets.

The tone of the game was set before the two teams had even stepped on the field. Wilson and his team had read the local papers and the PN-G Indians had some predictions. "Their kids were saying that Lamar had not played a team like them. How physical they were and how that would negate Lamar's speed. Actually, the truth could not have been more different. We prided ourselves on physicality." Lamar's defensive mantra was they kept hitting until their opponent got tired of it, and then they hit them some more. The game had been rated a toss-up by most pundits.

After the opening kickoff, something odd happened. The Mustang players running back to their sideline suddenly turned around to listen as the Indians were all chatter. It caught everybody's attention because the Lamar guys seemed a little stunned. Then the Mustang coaches yelled at their kids to get off the field. They huddled them and gave them a stern lecture. Wilson needed their full attention. "I told them to ignore all that trash talking. We were better than that and we were there to play a football game and nothing else. I told them to zip it."

The tactic was PN-G's way of letting the Mustangs know they would not be intimidated by the higher ranked team. With all the banter it became obvious it was going to be a long night. The Lamar crowd hoped the boys in blue kept their composure. Quarterback DJ Smallwood was not taking the bait. He saw it as a weak attempt to try and get in their heads. Lamar was not going to let that happen. The game was physical throughout for the junior QB and his offense. "Those guys were big and country and talked a lot. They played a little over the edge, but it just made us want to prove how physical we could be. We definitely responded."

Port Neches featured their powerful fullback Jake Hemmings who loved to relentlessly pound the line of scrimmage. Lamar linebacker Cory Green found the big Indian back a tough chore. "They had this big, strong running back who they just fed the ball to all game. He was very tough to tackle, and they blocked for him very well." PNG had some stumbles during the regular season. In their last game in district, they were smoked 40-7 by upstart Dayton who made it all the way to the 4A Semifinals before losing to eventual Division II champion Austin Lake Travis. But the Indians had put that in their rearview mirror. PN-G had its traditions and that good ole Indian pride.

The Indians used that late season loss to motivate themselves to prove they were not that bad. The next week they had met Galena Park in bi-district and, after a slow start, came roaring into the second half, scoring at will. They used the victory as a springboard into this contest. The defense was starting to believe they could shut down an offense as notable as Lamar's. The Indians came to Stallworth with renewed vigor. In the playoffs, each week is a fresh start.

The Mustangs received the opening kickoff and immediately looked to establish the running game. Setting up in the power I, they got the ball in Rodgers' hands immediately. He was stuffed on consecutive downs as the Indians brought everybody up close to the line of scrimmage to load the box. After an incomplete pass to wideout Travis Riedel the Mustangs were forced to punt. PN-G had set the tone on defense. Taylor Turner's punt was downed at the Indians' 47-yard line giving PN-G excellent starting field position.

The Indians were a triple option offense with quarterback Harrison Tatum under center, Hemings as the fullback and Joshua Wright the running back. Wright and Hemmings found some success early. At one point Hemmings crashed through the line of scrimmage carrying the ball down to the goal line. From there, Wright took the pitch from Tatum and outran everyone to the right side of the end zone for the game's first score. With 2:45 left in the first quarter the Indians had drawn first blood.

| INDIANS | 7 |
| MUSTANGS | 0 |

PN-G had indeed carried over the momentum from their win over Galena Park. They had come out and shut down the Lamar running attack and then put together a classic Indian grinding drive for an early lead. Now it was up to the Mustangs to respond after a lackluster start. Quizz brought the kickoff out to the Lamar 27-yard line. On first down he took a tite toss

and gashed thru several Indians on his way to the Lamar 46-yard line for a
first down. After a face-mask penalty against PN-G, Quizz took a delayed
handoff and sprinted to the Indian 32-yard line. The Indian defense was
getting an up close and personal showing on the cutting ability and acceleration of Jacquizz Rodgers.

It took a big completion from Smallwood to wideout DD Goodson to
keep the drive alive down to the Indian 21-yard line. Lamar continued to
operate out of a one back set to spread the Indian defense out some and keep
them from loading the box. The first quarter ended on a Smallwood keeper
to the PN-G fifteen. After the two teams switched sides of the field, Wilson
went back to the power I and kept feeding Quizz until the senior running
back found the end zone on a 10-yard scamper with 10:04 left in the second
quarter. Turner's PAT was good, and the contest was tied.

| INDIANS | 7 |
| MUSTANGS | 7 |

Whatever momentum PN-G might have gained in the first quarter had
suddenly evaporated. After Adan Gomez's kickoff, the Mustang defense came
out ready to get physical. The Indians continued to grind it, but a dead ball
personal foul for unnecessary roughness put them in a hole, and the hard-
running Hemmings could not bring them out. However, an offsides penalty
on linebacker Sule Osagiede bailed the Indians out on a failed third down
attempt. With Osagiede blitzing the middle relentlessly, the Indian offense
looked to their passing game to get some yardage. After several incompletions they were forced to punt. It was clear they would not be able to aban-
don their running attack against the much quicker Mustang secondary.

Hemmings' punt was downed at the Lamar 35-yard line where the Mustang offense set up once again in the power I. A misdirection run on first
down saw Quizz twist and weave his way to the PN-G 45-yard line. A holding penalty negated a first down scramble by Smallwood, but the junior signal caller came right back with a beautiful pass to Riedel who was interfered
with at the Indian 30-yard line. With a fresh set of downs, the Mustang
offensive line continued to move people out of the way and Quizz torched
the Indians for thirty more yards and a second touchdown. The point after

was missed and with 3:22 remaining in the half the Mustangs had gained the upper hand.

INDIANS	**7**
MUSTANGS	**13**

Gomez's kick was brought out to the Indian twenty-five and the pushing and banter continued after the whistle. Wilson reminded his players to not get involved in any of the trash talking or theatrics. With the option play still not working, the Indians once again went to the air, this time with some success. Quarterback Tatum found open receivers and moved the ball deep into Lamar territory. Mixing in an occasional run by Hemmings, the Indians found themselves at Lamar's 12-yard line. Then the massive Mustang defensive line took over.

First it was Clarence Ward who stuffed Hemmings for no gain. On second down, sophomore D'Vonn Brown came from his defensive end position to stop QB Tatum again for no gain. An errant high snap on third forced Tatum to throw the ball away and the Indians were called for holding, moving the ball back to the Mustang 32-yard line. On the repeat of third down, a blitzing Carlos Becerra caught Tatum back at the Lamar 39-yard line for another loss. On fourth and forever Wilson sent everybody and the kitchen sink on the blitz and the entire defensive line collapsed on Tatum for another loss. The promising offensive series for PN-G turned into a feeding frenzy by the Mustang defense and sent the two teams to the locker room with Lamar having all the momentum.

Halftime for the Mustangs was the same as usual. Coach Wilson never tried to do much outside of the original plan. There was rarely any halftime speech or anything else. Wilson always told the kids not to make the game bigger than it was. In the Indian locker room, coach Matt Burnett had to figure out how to slow down a surging Mustang offense, and also get his offense back on track. The Indians had been picked to finish no better than fifth in their district prior to the season so they had already surpassed most expectations. But Port Neches always had high expectations for their football teams, and this year was no different.

The Indians received the second half kickoff from Gomez and ran it back to their thirty for good starting position. As with Lamar, PN-G also prided themselves as a second half team. It was time to get Hemmings and company going. However, on second down Osagiede hit the gap and met Tatum just as he was attempting a pitch, knocking the ball back to the 19-yard line for a huge loss. Ward stuffed Hemmings on third and the Indians punted to the Lamar 42-yard line where the Mustang offense took over. On first down, Quizz took the pitch and burst through a big hole making his way to the PN-G 36-yard line. The Indian defense stiffened from there forcing a Lamar punt.

Tatum was unable to get his offense back on track and PN-G was forced to punt after a three and out. On second down from his own thirty-seven, Smallwood dropped back and fired down to the Indian 19-yard line where he connected with a streaking Travis Riedel for a huge completion. More importantly, the Indians had gone back to loading the box to stop Quizz and they had gotten burned by the big arm of Smallwood. From there the Mustangs went back to a steady diet of Rodgers who scored from eight yards out. Turner's PAT was good and Lamar Consolidated was sitting with a two-score lead at the 3:18 mark of the third quarter.

INDIANS	**7**
MUSTANGS	**20**

PN-G started at their own twenty after the touchback and Tatum managed to move his offense to midfield, aided by a defensive holding penalty. From there the drive stalled out. After another Indian punt, the Mustangs took over at their own 18-yard line. Smallwood continued to find Riedel and the senior wideout got up to the Mustang 35-yard line. The third quarter came to an end with the Mustangs firmly in control of the regional contest.

The Mustang offense then went on a time-consuming drive that mixed in some nifty scrambles and throws by Smallwood along with the power running of Rodgers. However, a holding penalty negated a big run by Rodgers and, on third and long, Smallwood threw into the end zone where the Indians intercepted. Needing to score quickly, coach Burnett went to the airways. Tatum used an accurate arm to move the ball into Mustang territory. Once again though, Mustang defensive coordinator Wade dialed up the defensive pressure and Tatum no longer had time to throw. The ball went over on downs on another incomplete pass.

Smallwood brought his offense to the line at midfield, needing only to bleed the clock at this point. After several solid runs by Quizz, Smallwood went back to Riedel deep in PN-G territory for a first and ten at the Indian 27-yard line. On second down, Quizz gashed the middle for twenty-five yards and his fourth score of the game. Now the Indians were in real trouble with very little time left.

INDIANS	**7**
MUSTANGS	**26**

Tatum went no huddle and tried once more with the passing game. But once again the Mustangs pinned their ears back and came charging on every snap. Things began to heat up and tempers flared. After holding their tongues for most of the contest, the Mustangs players started responding to the barbs thrown at them. Three unsportsmanlike penalties against Lamar kept the Indians alive after several incomplete passes. The game had turned ugly. With first and ten at the Lamar 14-yard line, the Indians had one last chance to score. However, D'Vonn Brown chased Tatum down from behind back at the twenty and time expired. The Mustang fans were excited, but probably more relieved. There still were a lot of questions about how good Consolidated really was.

Hemmings knew the Indians had let this one get away early. "We got out of the gate okay, but then we had too many costly penalties and, unfortunately, some of our key players didn't have a good game. It couldn't have come at a worse time. I certainly could have played better, but hats off to those guys. They played their butts off."

After the cake walk they had against Dickinson, this contest proved a little tougher. Austin LBJ had defeated Houston Furr 57-16 in their regional matchup, setting up a quarterfinal game against Lamar the following week. The site was set at Kyle Field, the home of the Texas A&M Aggies in College Station. The Mustangs could not afford a slow start against the Jaguars who were big and physical, much like the Mustangs themselves. Still, the Mustangs were moving on. The plan remained intact.

CHAPTER 10

GOD'S COUNTRY

Austin LBJ Jaguars

Thanksgiving 2007 lasted only half the day. The players reported for practice at 2:00 in the afternoon. As the team emerged from the locker room at Traylor Stadium, one could only imagine how much turkey and dressing had been consumed by that bunch. If there is one thing high school boys can do better than anything else, it's eating. Coach Wilson gathered his players at midfield and went to work. After about fifteen minutes, Coach Velasquez strolled over to the home stands where about ten or so parents were seated to watch practice. As Velasquez approached each one, he asked the same question. "Who you with?" As the parents shouted out their sons' names, Velasquez gave each one a smile and a thumbs up. He was checking for anybody who did not belong. No spies that day.

As practice was wrapping up, Wilson pulled out another teaching moment. This time it was field goal kicker Adan Gomez's turn. After running a spirit sprint, Wilson had the field goal unit line up for a 35-yard attempt. It was simple; make it and huddle up. Miss it and run. Once again Wilson paused before passing the ball to Rohde. He took the moment to look his guys in the eyes. One by one. No words were needed. Osagiede led the rhythmic claps. The encouraging words poured out. The snap from Rohde to Becerra was crisp and on target. The hold was solid, and Gomez booted it solid down the middle.

The Agricultural and Mechanical College of Texas opened in 1876 as a part of the land grant colleges under the provisions of the Morrill Land-Grant

Acts. Originally it was an all-male institute and all students were members of the corps of cadets, an ROTC program. Eventually it became a university, admitting both male and female students and making the corps voluntary. The football team claims three national championships, but the school is most famous for being known as the "Home of the 12th man" in reference to the game whereby Aggie basketball player E. King Gill came out of the stands to suit up for a short-handed football squad. Having spent four years of undergraduate there and then four more years in the College of Veterinary Medicine, I was well indoctrinated into the traditions of Aggieland.

Kyle Field is the stadium the Aggies play football in as part of the Southeastern Conference. Built in 1927 and named in recognition of Edwin Jackson Kyle, the stadium is part of the rich history of Texas A&M. When I began my time at TAMU in 1980, we were not winning very many football games. But then Jackie Sherrill came to town and things changed. One improvement was that Kevin Murray decided to put his professional baseball career on hold to finally accept his offer to play football at TAMU. The next thing you knew, we were packing the hallowed Cotton Bowl watching Murray lead our Aggies to a huge upset win over Heisman winner Bo Jackson and his Auburn Tigers. We finally were relevant and would remain so for a long time. So it goes without saying that a huge smile crossed my face when it was announced that the Lamar Consolidated Mustangs would be playing their next playoff game in Kyle Field.

The drive up Highway 6 to College Station is always serene. There is nothing but farm and ranch land on both sides of the highway. The signs read "Alfalfa for Sale by the Bale" and "Certified Red Brangus Cattle". The fields are full of cows, tractors, and old broken down farm trucks long since abandoned. It is what they refer to in Texas as "pure country." There probably is a country song to that effect.

After putting away Port Neches-Groves 26-7 in Regional play, the Mustangs met up against the Austin LBJ Jaguars in the Quarterfinals for a chance to advance to the Semi-Finals as they had done the previous season. The Jaguars had begun their playoff run with a tough 20-18 bi-district win over the highly state ranked Brenham Cubs. Like the Mustangs, LBJ's season had not been a cakewalk.

After starting the season with a 21-6 win over Cameron Yoe, the Jaguars stumbled badly against Del Valle, losing 25-7. They then went on a five-game winning streak against some lesser opponents that saw them scoring upwards of seventy points in a couple of games. They came back down to earth in week eight with a surprising loss to Manor, losing 19-13. They collected themselves for a strong finish with a 35-21 victory over Elgin and a 41-14 thrashing of Travis. Much like Lamar, LBJ had a season of ups and downs where they could look lights out some times and lost at others.

Lyndon Baines Johnson was named President of the United States of America on November 22, 1963, following the assassination of John F. Kennedy in Dallas, Texas. Johnson had served as the U. S. senator from Texas prior to joining the Kennedy ticket after being unsuccessful in his own bid for the presidency. Johnson was well known in the Senate after he spearheaded the passage of the Civil Rights Acts of 1957 and 1960. Johnson was remembered for his heroic stance on civil rights and his anguish over the loss of lives in the Vietnam War. A Texan at heart, Johnson spent a lot of time at his ranch outside of Austin. So naturally when it came time for his presidential library to be established, Austin was the obvious choice. And in 1974, the Lyndon Baines Johnson high school was built in Austin and named for the late president. The school colors selected were purple and white and the Jaguar was chosen as their mascot.

Going into the 2006 football season, Dave Campbell's Texas Football had the Brenham Cubs ranked second in the state in 4A behind Texarkana Texas High. Likewise, the 2007 Brenham squad was highly touted, having kept most of its star players. LBJ coach Claude Mathis knew the road to a championship would mean getting past a veteran Brenham Cubs squad that had gone deep into the playoffs the previous year. In 2006 the Cubs advanced to the Quarterfinals only to lose to Texas City who then lost to district rival and eventual state champion La Marque. Brenham, with its stingy defense, knew they could hang with just about anybody in Class 4A if their offense could score enough points. Their first test in the 2007 playoffs would be their bi-district contest against Austin's LBJ at Viking Stadium in Bryan, Texas. Looking at the right side of the Division I playoff bracket, many pundits penciled Brenham into the championship game slot.

Led by team captain Kyle Mangan, their 6'2" 220-pound stud inside linebacker, the Cubs were accustomed to handling some of the better offenses in the state. Plus, the Cubs were coming in on a seven-game winning streak and felt they were finally hitting their stride after a couple of early season non-district losses. Mangan had already committed to Texas A&M but was hungry to finish the job in high school and go out on a positive note. And

Brenham did not appreciate the low state ranking after being so dominant in 2006. Mangan and his teammates were mad and felt they needed to prove the media wrong. They lost a lot of D-1 guys to graduation, but still had eight to nine guys who were considered D-1 prospects. At first the Brenham defense found success stuffing LBJ's Derrick Grant and running back Ed Middleton, and pressuring starting quarterback Devarus Wright. Brenham took a 2-0 lead after a safety against LBJ.

It was at this point that Coach Mathis made a change that ultimately turned the tide of the game. Knowing that the Cub defense would continue doubling up on Grant, Mathis inserted backup quarterback Curtis Parks Jr. into the game. Mathis had his game plan ready for anything. He had planned on playing both quarterbacks anyway. "Brenham was worried about Derrick Grant to the point of double-teaming him."

A bigger and stronger Parks became a second running option and one that proved problematic for Mangan and his defense. "We really did not know a lot about LBJ. We knew they had a couple of D-1 guys, most notably Cavanaugh and Grant. Grant was our focus."

Brenham head coach Glen West knew that Wright was a better thrower but was not as physical of a runner as Parks. His defense gave LBJ fits early on. "We thought we could handle the run game and gave Grant extra attention. Then Parks came in right before the half, and he did a good job keeping our defense honest with QB keepers." Coach West had seen a lot of that in recent seasons, where teams were going to that kind of quarterback that did it all. It would become an underlying theme to the Class 4A Division 1 playoffs in 2007.

Parks knew of the likelihood he would be inserted into the game at some point, and he knew LBJ had an advantage there. Coach Mathis had put a lot of emphasis on everybody, including Parks, needing to be prepared mentally. Brenham had scouted LBJ the week before but didn't get any film on Parks in particular. Mathis knew this and had Parks ready.

With Parks taking over under center the LBJ offense came to life, driving fifty-seven yards to Brenham's own 8-yard line with time running out. But Parks was hit hard by Mangan before crossing the goal line and fumbled into the Cubs' end zone where Brenham recovered it for a touchback. It looked as though Brenham would take a slim 2-0 lead into the locker room at halftime, but Cubs quarterback Kyler Crenshaw threw the first of his three interceptions that LBJ defender Anthony Nichols returned to the Cubs' own 10-yard line. Parks scored with twenty-two seconds left in the half. A muffed snap ended the attempted extra point, and LBJ headed to the locker room leading 6-2 and with a renewed confidence that would carry them in the second half.

The Jaguars got another interception early in the third quarter that led to a touchdown pass from Parks to Grant. Erasmo Castro's point after was good to give LBJ a 13-2 lead. Brenham later recorded its second safety of the game when Mangan caught Wright, who had re-entered the game, in the end zone. Mangan had his hunches on the play. "I read it correctly and shot the gap untouched to catch Wright in the end zone."

Crenshaw breathed new life into the Cubs' offense with a 55-yard touchdown pass to cut LBJ's lead to 13-11. However, the Jaguars got back on a roll with Parks back in and scored once again to go up 20-11. Brenham made it close after another LBJ turnover, closing the gap to 20-18 which was the final score. LBJ escaped the bi-district contest, proving once again they had a legitimate defense, but more importantly, they now had a new offensive weapon to use against their next opponent, Houston Furr.

This new wrinkle presented Lamar Coach Lydell Wilson with another problem to worry about. LBJ had overcome two safeties and a lost fumble into the end zone, which had Mathis and his defensive coordinator pulling their hair out. "My defensive coordinator said just punt as our defense had this, and don't do anything stupid." If nothing else, the Brenham contest prepared LBJ for what awaited them down the road. They now knew they could play a tough, close game, and come out on top.

As the Mustangs neared the stadium, they could see the Kyle Field lights from George Bush Drive. The Lamar crowd was seated on the A&M student side in the lower deck. Across the field were the purple and white clad Jaguars. And yes, they were big and intimidating. Mathis similarly looked across Kyle Field and had some concerns of his own. Lamar had the best running back in the state and Smallwood had to be accounted for as well. Mathis thought Lamar's defense was good but could be exposed. He planned on putting as many hats on Rodgers as possible when on defense and showing multiple sets and personnel packages when on offense. After warm-ups, Osagiede was back on his stationary bicycle.

Mathis needed just enough offense to balance his stellar defense. But his offensive game plan had changed somewhat due to Parks getting injured the previous week against Furr. LBJ needed to get the ball in Derrick Grant's hands any way possible and get him in space. It was a tight game throughout with Quizz having a hard time finding running room as well. LBJ had their main man on a mission. Mathis knew linebacker Ricky Cavanaugh, the Class 4A Defensive Player of the Year, would keep the Jaguars in the game. He was more concerned about his young cornerback. Lining up next to Cavanaugh was another solid linebacker in Barlow Davis. The tandem absolutely loved causing mayhem with opposing offenses. LBJ was the only team Lamar faced in 2007 that matched their size and physicality. It turned out to be the slugfest predicted.

Before the game started there was a controversy of sorts. As Quizz went through warmups, he noticed a referee and several unidentified gentlemen approach Coach Wilson. The conversation seemed intense as Wilson shook his head several times and argued with the gentlemen. Then Wilson turned and yelled for Quizz to come to the sideline. At this point, Osagiede grabbed at Quizz's #33 jersey and inquired what was happening. Quizz could only pull away and walk towards the Mustang bench. His mind raced, but he remained clueless. Wilson instructed Rodgers to sit on the trainer's table. The small group that had assembled began inspecting Rodgers' cleats which were heavily taped as usual. Wilson informed Quizz that an objection had been filed against the type of cleats he was wearing. Here it was again. Quizz couldn't help but roll his eyes.

Are you kidding me?

It was just one more obstacle thrown against the kid from the Heights. Rodgers didn't care as he sat stone-faced. They could try anything they wanted, but they would never succeed in knocking him off balance. Running backs coach Ronnie Humphrey knew the challenge against Rodgers was bogus. The Kyle Field folks and the LBJ coaching staff objected to the length of Rodgers' cleats. It was determined that the cleats were legal. In Humphrey's mind, the ploy was just something to distract Lamar. "It was so obvious that it was laughable. But that's football and it's the playoffs."

Smallwood, Rodgers, Obi, and Osagiede walked to midfield for the coin toss in their traveling white uniforms. Cavanaugh, Davis, left tackle Manny Rodriquez, and center Colin Buggs represented LBJ wearing their home purple uniforms. The Jaguar fans were seated in the former students side of the stadium and the Mustang faithful were on the students side. Across the stadium from the Lamar fans was an LBJ sign in the stands that read **JAC-QUIZZ CONSOLIDATED**. It seemed unfair, but at the same time, not so far-fetched. They at least had made their intentions known: stop Rodgers.

The Jaguars opening drive saw Wright in the shotgun. However, just before the snap Wright shifted to his right and Grant slid into the Wildcat position behind center. Mathis was trying to get his best offensive athlete going early. Mathis had started putting Grant in the shotgun in the first round of the playoffs. The wildcat had worked well for him and LBJ. But the Mustang defense sniffed it out and the play went for a one-yard gain. The tone for this game was set. A lot of good defense and offenses trying any and everything to get their best players in space. Grant was able to break outside on the next play, and then running back Ed Middleton got going.

Mixing up their rotation and keeping the Mustangs guessing was LBJ's early game plan. For a while it seemed to work as the Jaguars quickly moved past midfield. But then the pressure from the Mustang defensive front and a slashing Osagiede forced Wright into making some hurried throws. The ball went over on downs and Lamar had excellent starting position at its own forty-two. Early penalties put the Mustangs in a hole and on fourth down they punted back to LBJ.

Mathis then substituted in Parks and tried to get running back Omasha Brantley going. He still occasionally put Grant in the Wildcat. Once again LBJ was across midfield, but the Mustangs were gunning for the run. Parks, who was limited in passing due to a separated shoulder in his throwing arm, found the going tough. Mathis answered by putting Wright back in and went to his aerial attack. Wright hit Grant at the Lamar thirty for the deepest penetration of the game. But on fourth and ten Wright threw into the end zone for an incompletion. Grant saw that Lamar was intent on keeping him covered up in obvious passing situations. "They had an extra defender on my side to take away any chance of an inside route."

The Mustang offense set up at their own thirty. The Jaguar defensive front and linebacking corps, led by Davis and Cavanaugh, had effectively taken Quizz out of the game thus far. After getting stuffed yet again on first down, Wilson went rather early to his special play for this game. Each week the Mustang coaches would throw in a new play that was specific for the team they were playing in case they needed to do something different. They would name these plays for the mascot of the opposing team. In the case of LBJ, they had a particular new play code-named "Jaguar". It entailed getting Quizz into the pass pattern in the event that Mathis overloaded the box on defense. Once it became obvious that LBJ was ignoring the pass, a frustrated Rodgers approached his head coach. Wilson knew it was time to break out his special play for the game.

Mathis, who was busy on the sideline with his offensive line, saw the play develop too late. He was making adjustments with the O-line and happen to see Quizz go in motion from the backfield. He knew immediately where that was going. Mathis could not get a timeout called. On that play Lamar quarterback DJ Smallwood hit Quizz in stride for a 70-yard touchdown along the Jaguar sideline. Mathis was beside himself. "I stopped calling offensive plays after that game. I should have been paying attention to my defense. But the game was far from over at that point." Taylor Turner's point after kick was good and, with forty-four seconds left in the opening quarter, Lamar was on the board.

AUSTIN LBJ	0
LAMAR CONS	7

On its next series LBJ went three and out. The Jaguars' strategy of pooch punting to avoid a Rodgers return gave the Mustang offense first and ten at its own 43-yard line. Lamar was looking to continue the momentum they had now established. Cavanaugh and his defense had other plans, and the Jaguars continued to shut down the Lamar running attack. After three and out, the Mustangs punted again. On the ensuing punt, Lamar dodged a bullet. LBJ's Grant took the punt at his own thirty and broke free for a touchdown. However, the play was nullified by several penalties including a block in the back. Lamar had seen all of Derrick Grant that they cared to. They went to the pooch punt to the sideline from that point on.

Coach Wilson received a second scare on the punt return. Osagiede had been hit on his sore knee. As Wilson watched his trainers attend to his star linebacker, he said a small prayer. Losing his captain would not only be a blow to his defense, it would also break a young man's heart. It was often Osagiede's spirit of competition that carried this team emotionally. Not being able to finish would crush the young Nigerian.

After a couple of plays, Osagiede returned to his command post behind the defensive line. LBJ was unable to move the ball and had to punt. However, Lamar got called for a roughing the punter penalty which gave the ball back to LBJ at their own 30-yard line with five minutes remaining in the half. On first down, Middleton was off to the races, crossing the 50-yard line. LBJ had lost Brantley and Grant to ankle injuries. Brantley had come into this contest banged up. Mathis had hoped he could keep both Parks and Brantley on the field. Now it was obvious that was not going to happen. It was up to Wright and Middleton to make something happen.

The Jaguars continued working the option down the field. A big third down pass from Wright to receiver Jeremy Moore set the Jaguars up with a first and goal at the Lamar four with time running out in the first half. Middleton finished off the drive with a score. Erasmo Castro's point after was good and, with just 1:33 remaining in the half, the score was all tied up.

AUSTIN LBJ	**7**
LAMAR CONS	**7**

The Mustangs quickly moved down the field on long runs by Quizz and Smallwood, but the drive ended with an LBJ interception at the Jaguar's own 4-yard line. The half was over, and Lamar had blown a golden opportunity. Mistakes, penalties, and mental lapses so far had ruled the day. There was a very good chance that something unexpected could determine the outcome of this contest. In the locker rooms, there really was not much to do as far as making adjustments. It was a matter of finding what worked on offense and to continue hard-nosed defense. It was going to be a war of wills the rest of the way.

Just before the half, Grant limped off the field. As the trainers attended to their star it was obvious his ankle was bothering him. He was unable to stand on the sideline during the last couple of minutes of the half. In the LBJ stands, a concerned Derrick Grant Sr. and his wife looked on as their son hobbled to the locker room. They soon were on their feet headed down to the check things out. In the locker room Derrick Jr. saw the anguish on his parents' faces. "Instead of going over stuff with the coaching staff, I spent the halftime discussing with my parents if I could return. It became obvious I was out." The loss of Grant was especially tough for LBJ because he played such a crucial role on offense, defense, and special teams.

With twenty-four minutes left, or so they thought, the two teams exited their locker rooms looking to take the next step and advance to the semi-finals. In the other quarterfinal matchup, undefeated New Braunfels was taking on Gregory Portland. Lamar received the second half kickoff. Wanting to keep the ball out of Rodgers hands, Mathis had Castro pooch kick towards the Mustang sideline. The ball went out of bounds and Lamar elected to take it at their own thirty-one for good starting position. As he approached the offensive huddle, Quizz immediately noticed one glaring fact. And so did Wilson and the entire Lamar coaching staff. Derrick Grant was not in his starting cornerback position. A spot where he literally dictated what opposing offenses could and couldn't do. Instead, Grant stood on the Jaguar sideline without shoulder pads. His face was screwed tight. His gaze went nowhere. His lips remained pursed as he fought the tears of disappointment. This was the second half. This was the time he made the game his. Now, he had been rendered a spectator. And his only hope was that LBJ could survive this night and give his swollen ankle a chance to heal.

Cavanaugh and his defense continued to focus on Rodgers. With seven to eight men in the box Mathis was not going to allow Quizz to get out of the gate in this second half. On first down Quizz squirted through to the 42-yard line of Lamar for a quick first down. Then LBJ shut down the run. On third down Smallwood rolled to his right looking for wideout Travis Riedel on the sideline. However, the Jaguars picked him off at their own forty-eight. It was another costly mistake in this tight contest. The Jaguar offense was quickly on the field looking to resume the momentum they had taken into halftime. Mathis sent out both quarterbacks along with Middleton in the backfield. It was one of many offensive sets he used in the contest.

On first down Wright handed to Middleton and the speedy back got into the open down the middle to the Lamar twenty-six. It was not the start the Mustang defense had hoped for. Then the Lamar defense stiffened, and Mathis sent in Castro for a field goal attempt of forty yards. Just before the snap Mathis called timeout and decided to go for a first down. His instincts told him to strike while he had the momentum. Out came Wright who set up in the shotgun with an empty set. The junior signal caller coolly stepped up into the pocket and hit a wide-open Moore who made it all the way to the two-yard line for first and goal. The gamble had paid off. On the next play Middleton got his second touchdown of the night, and the LBJ faithful started rocking the stadium. Castro's point after was good and, with 7:58 remaining in the third quarter, Lamar head coach Wilson needed some answers on both offense and defense.

AUSTIN LBJ	**14**
LAMAR CONS	**7**

Lamar started their next drive at their own thirty-five. On second down Smallwood put Rodgers in motion out of the backfield and fired to his senior running back for a gain to the Lamar 43-yard line. Wilson had to do whatever it took to get Quizz with the ball in space. Both head coaches were willing to try any and everything to move the chains. From there the drive bogged down. Cavanaugh and Barlow were relentless in their attack. Lamar was forced to punt.

On second down Middleton appeared to get the corner to his left, but Chuck Obi flashed in suddenly to stop him for a two-yard gain. LBJ ended up punting and Lamar was in excellent field position at the Jaguar 38-yard line. With Grant out of the game, the Mustangs could now load the box. Back on offense, Wilson went to his power I, and Quizz responded with some hard runs to move the chains. Mathis in turn responded by putting eight men in the box, and the move worked as the ball went over on downs. However, another costly penalty against LBJ moved the ball back to their own twelve where their offense set up shop. Then a chop block moved the ball half the distance to the LBJ 6-yard line. Mistakes continued to pile up for both teams.

The Jaguars eventually punted, and Lamar again started at midfield looking desperate to get something going. A counter to Quizz on first down moved the ball to the LBJ 40-yard line and time expired in the third stanza. LBJ stiffened to start the fourth quarter, and Lamar was looking at a third and long back at midfield. Wilson went empty set with Smallwood in the shotgun. Out to his right was Rodgers. This time the Jaguars were not fooled, and Rodgers was double teamed. Smallwood took the snap, set his feet, and fired towards the LBJ sideline. Quizz got behind the two defenders and at the last second made an adjustment on the ball. He somehow made a behind the back catch and fell at the 15-yard line. On the next play, Quizz took the pitch from Smallwood and exploded through the left side of the line where Beny Bravo and Jose Pena had opened up a huge hole. Rodgers tucked in behind his tight end, Dominique Briggs, and was quickly into the end zone. Adan Gomez's point after tied the game with 10:48 to play.

| AUSTIN LBJ | 14 |
| LAMAR CONS | 14 |

With most of the fourth quarter remaining, there was still plenty of time left in this contest for each team to make something happen. Mathis sent out Parks to see if he could run the ball for a sustained drive and milk some clock. Parks was ready. After moving quickly to their own forty, the Jaguar offense ran into a stubborn Mustang defense that had rallied around their leader Osagiede. The relentless Nigerian prince was tackling sideline to sideline. Mathis was forced to go back with Wright and the pass.

The Mustang secondary was in shut down mode, and on third down free safety Steven Fleming batted away another Wright pass intended for Jaguar receiver Regis Wilson, forcing the Jaguars to punt from midfield. On top of this, Mathis was losing one player after another to injuries. The hard-hitting contest had taken its toll on the boys in purple. Rodgers saw the injuries piling up and knew it was affecting the Jaguar's performance. "They were dropping like flies. You never want to see anybody get hurt, and they were still very much in the game."

Starting at their own 30-yard line, the Mustang offense still had over four minutes to get a score. On first down, Rodgers took the pitch from Smallwood and scooted down the left sideline for a quick first down. Rodgers speed and elusiveness were starting to take over. He had been a second half running back all season and this game was no different. On second down, he powered through the middle to the forty-five of Lamar. Cavanaugh burst through to drop Quizz for a big loss on the next down, but Smallwood answered by firing a strike to Travis Riedel at the Lamar forty-eight. Riedel shrugged off the Jaguar corner and was run out at the LBJ 35-yard line for a huge first down. Here, once again, the absence of Grant was hurting the Jaguars.

On first down, Smallwood handed to Quizz who was immediately met by the surging LBJ front line. He hit the brakes, juked to his left, and cut through to the second level. Another juke to the outside, and he hit the Lamar sideline to his left. There, he was boxed in by two Jaguars. He cut back again and raced towards the center of the field. Using a vicious stiff-arm he fought his way to the 2-yard line. It was vintage Jacquizz Rodgers all of the way, and Lamar was on the precipice of taking a lead with precious little time left in regulation. Except that there was a little yellow hanky laying on the Kyle Field turf back at the 35-yard line. Holding was called against the Mustangs. The LBJ faithful breathed a collective sigh of relief. On the Mustang side, there was total disbelief. Yards had come at a premium all night. Finally, Quizz was able to do his thing and it was all for naught.

The untimely penalty moved the ball all of the way back to the LBJ 45-yard line. If anything, this call squared the two teams for the Grant punt return in the first half. Chances were not good that LBJ would have stopped the Mustangs with first and goal at the two. On top of that, there would have been almost no time left in regulation for the Jaguar offense to score. The Mustangs tried desperately to connect on a long ball near the goal line but only came away with incompletions. On fourth down, they were too far to attempt a field goal and had to punt. Mathis played it conservatively and regulation ended with the game tied up 14-14.

In overtime, both teams had an offensive series from the 25-yard line. The Mustangs went on offense first. Coming out in their basic power I formation, they felt they had some momentum at the end of regulation and hoped it would carry over. At this point LBJ had an equal amount of resolve. The Mustangs went back to the same play they had just scored with, but this time Cavanaugh and Davis were waiting and stopped Quizz for no gain. On second down, Smallwood threw incomplete in the left flat to Riedel. He was flushed out of the pocket on third down and made it to the 17-yard line, leaving Wilson with a big decision.

During pre-game, the Lamar coaches had watched both Turner and Gomez kick both with and against the wind. Wilson made his decision then. It was decided that if a field goal were needed then Taylor would kick it if it was with the wind, and Gomez would kick it if it was into the wind. As it turned out, Lamar was looking at a 34-yard try into the wind. It would be the left-footed Gomez. The fact that the junior kicker was there at all was somewhat of a fluke.

Gomez had come close to never playing football. He was a soccer player, and kicked a football for the first time in PE in eighth grade. It got him curious about the sport. He wanted to go to freshman football camp, but his brother did not want to take him because the varsity had gone 2-8 the year before, and had developed a bad reputation. Once there, Gomez told the freshman coaches that he just wanted to be a kicker, but they did not listen and put him with the linemen. Gomez had to wait until after practice to show his kicking skills. Now he was about to attempt the biggest kick in his still young life.

The junior put his spot for holder Carlos Becerra at the 24-yard line. He counted his steps and nodded his head. The snap and hold were perfect, and Gomez booted the ball towards the goal post. He bent down and picked up his tee before the ball ever crossed the goal line. A good kicker knows immediately based on feel. Gomez knew this one was right down the middle with plenty of distance.

AUSTIN LBJ	**14**
LAMAR CONS	**17**

Now it would be up to the Lamar defense to keep the Mustangs' hopes alive by keeping LBJ out of the end zone. Outside linebacker Chuck Obi came alive in the OT. On first down, Obi shot the gap and threw LBJ running back Ed Middleton for a four-yard loss. On second down, Middleton tried the right side and ran into Clarence Ward and Deante Ester for one yard. Mathis then called a pass play on third down, but Devarus Wright was pressured by a blitzing Obi and his attempt fell incomplete. Now the Jaguars were looking at a decision to try and tie the game or go for the first down.

On the Jaguar sideline, a disgusted Derrick Grant stood with a grimace on his face. It was not because of the pain shooting through his ankle but because of the hurt piercing his heart. LBJ never knew for sure if they could be title contenders. Now, Grant knew, and he was not there to help when his team needed him most. Curtis Parks Jr., likewise, stood nearby with thoughts of what should have been. He had been so explosive against Brenham before his shoulder separation. He also could only look on and wonder how this could have gone differently. Maybe they get out of this place with a win and he, Brantley, and Grant could get healthy quickly.

Mathis sent Jaguar kicker Erasmo Castro out to attempt a 39-yard kick. It was going to be a long kick for his field goal unit, but Mathis was limited on offense and needed to stay alive long enough to figure this one out. The kick sailed left into the end zone where Lamar's Rodgers fielded it, ran to the five, and slid down. Game over.

AUSTIN LBJ	14
LAMAR CONS	17

The Lamar fans roared even though they were emotionally exhausted. The Jaguar side was quiet. Mothers, fathers, brothers, and sisters had made the drive to see their guys continue their journey. Now they sat, some shaking their heads in disbelief while others wiped tears. After having played so well coming into the contest, they had high expectations. The pundits in the media had practically promised them a win. There had been so many swings in momentum. Both teams had dodged catastrophe. It was difficult to watch the season end for the Jaguar faithful. This was one of the games where nobody really lost. But somebody had to move on, and somebody had to go home.

Parks remembers the game overall was the most physical he had ever played in, and on top of that, he had the untimely injury. "The game was tougher for me personally because I had sustained a separated shoulder. Plus, I believe they were more prepared for the times I was in the game. Obviously, they had watched a lot of film from Brenham or after."

Likewise, Cavanaugh saw his team being affected by injuries. "It was a war from start to finish. Maybe if we had been a little healthier, things might have turned out differently. There's no doubt losing DJ (Grant) so early hurt us. You can't lose your number one offensive threat. You know… the games that year in the playoffs were so close across the board, several teams could have won that title. It was a fun season and I hated seeing it end." Cavanaugh had to take consolation in the fact that he would be back on this same playing surface in the fall, adorned in Aggie maroon.

In the end, both teams walked off knowing they had left everything on the field. Although Quizz was held to 115 yards rushing on twenty-eight carries, he more than made up for that with 112 yards receiving on four receptions. The overtime experience would serve the Mustangs well going into their semi-final contest the following week against undefeated New Braunfels who had beaten Gregory Portland 38-14. Coach Mathis left the field with nothing but admiration for Jacquizz Rodgers. "I just have a lot of respect for that young man because he didn't back down from anyone and always brought it. He was CLUTCH!"

Lamar linebacker Carlos Becerra was impressed with the Jaguars' athleticism. "For me, LBJ was our hardest opponent, definitely the most athletic and talented team during our playoff run." The knockdown, drag-out victory had matured these Mustangs. They now had the confidence to take on all comers. The overtime experience would also come in handy very soon. Coach Wilson reflects. "I think attitudes about our team changed after Dickinson, as far as the media pundits went. But for me, it was that game against LBJ when I felt our guys were now battle tested. I knew that nothing would rattle them from then on out."

As Rodney Williams walked down the exit ramp leaving Kyle Field, he also started feeling some confidence again. Winning district had been expected. But this win required the Mustangs to overcome some serious talent on the other side of the ball. The Mustangs showed some character in maintaining their composure after falling behind. Lesser teams tended to crumble when losing a lead in the second half. Not this bunch.

Then Williams received more good news. Oregon State had played a favored Oregon Duck team in the annual Civil War. The game had gone into double overtime. James Rodgers ran a fly sweep for a touchdown in the second OT to give the Beavers a huge upset win. There would be some celebrating back in Richmond, Texas on this Saturday night. As Tasha Williams received the news from her brother, she pumped her fist and screamed. But something inside of her was churning. No time to relax now. Her baby's dream was more alive than ever. Now the New Braunfels Unicorns would try to steal that dream.

CHAPTER 11

ANOTHER SEMI-FINAL

New Braunfels Unicorns

When the town of New Braunfels is mentioned in Texas the most likely question heard is: "You gonna float down the Guadalupe? Or the Comal?" That's if it is summertime. In November, the big thing is Wurstfest, which is akin to the German Oktoberfest celebration in other places. The Guadalupe River starts in West Texas and runs down to Canyon Lake near New Braunfels. From there it winds its way down to spill into San Antonio Bay, which lies south of Port O'Conner. San Antonio Bay is one of many inter-coastal lakes along the Gulf of Mexico.

The part of the river that gets the most attention is what pours out of Canyon Lake. This is where droves of people like to put their canoes and inner tubes into the water and drift down the limestone banks of a sometimes fast-moving river. Near the town of New Braunfels, these groups of floaters can appear to be a huge continuous carpet of people weaving their way downstream. Occasionally there are tubes bound together around a community ice chest full of cold beverages. It's a popular destination for spring breakers.

In town near the city park are several large buildings: beer halls, that are open only for a short period in November for the Wurstfest celebration. The German influence is thick there as the townsfolk are adorned in full costume, dancing to live Polka music, eating sausages and bratwurst, and swigging beer from a stein. People travel from all over the state and country to attend this traditional celebration. The motels are booked a year in advance by the true devotees. For the most part, the citizens of New Braunfels welcome the visitors as the tradition is part of their heritage and brings in tourist dollars.

Another thing New Braunfels is known for in Texas is being highly competitive in high school football. I remember going to the Houston Astrodome in 1997 for the Class 5A Division II semifinals where the Unicorns were heavily overmatched against a much bigger and more athletic Alief Hastings team. Unicorn quarterback Kliff Kingsbury spent most of the night either scrambling or finding himself on his backside. Still, it was obvious he was the best player on the Astrodome turf that evening.

Kingsbury went on to star at Texas "Wreck-em" Tech University and eventually found himself as offensive coordinator at Texas A&M where he coached Johnny Manziel on the way to a Heisman Trophy. Kingsbury was lured back to Lubbock as head coach where he mentored Patrick Mahomes II, the Super Bowl winning quarterback of the Kansas City Chiefs. Kingsbury parlayed all of this success into the head coaching job for the NFL Arizona Cardinals.

The week leading up to the game against New Braunfels had the Mustang coaching staff intensely studying the complex Unicorn offense. Although the LBJ squad had matched the Mustangs in physicality, New Braunfels presented a different set of problems. For one, they had a more sophisticated offensive scheme that was possible due the veteran leadership they had that year. Much like the Mustangs, the Unicorns had figured to go further in the playoffs in 2006. Unlike the Mustangs, they had not been decimated by graduation. Their undefeated record thus far in 2007 came as a surprise to no one, including Head Coach Chuck Caniford and his star Quarterback, senior Ryan Perez.

Once again, the Mustangs' practice on Thursday ended with a teaching moment. This time Wilson had something different in mind. He needed this team razor-sharp focused. He needed them locked in. Wilson quietly instructed his center, Alex Rohde, to intentionally hike the ball over quarterback Smallwood's head to create a busted play. The move caught Smallwood off guard, but the junior gathered the loose ball quickly and salvaged a few yards. Wilson announced his trick and exhorted his guys to be ready for any and everything. Quizz and DJ could not help but smile at each other… Wilson never stopped coaching. Swag.

The Unicorns started the season ranked at number 11 by *Texas Football* magazine. Going into their contest with Lamar Consolidated they had steadily climbed up to the number two spot behind Copperas Cove in the rankings. As payback from a playoff loss in 2006, they plastered Alamo Heights 35-3 in their Regional matchup. They escaped a tough Quarterfinal contest with Gregory-Portland 27-23, keeping their undefeated dream season alive. Now they came into their semi-final game as a slight favorite over a battle-tested Mustang team that many experts still had questions about.

Looking down on the field during warm-ups, I spied Perez in his #6 royal blue jersey. He was throwing passes along the New. Braunfels sideline. So, that was the guy creating all of the hoopla by the media. I could tell by his stance and passing stroke that he was awash in confidence. Watching Perez led me to search out the Mustang defensive linemen. They were down in the north end zone doing their pregame stretching. They were the ones given the task of not letting Perez crush the Mustangs' dream. Brown, Nwaog-wugwu, Ester, Ward, Usen, and Quintanilla. I couldn't help but size them up, wondering if they had any idea what was about to be unleashed on them.

Coach Caniford had his team ready for what they would face on both sides of the ball against Lamar Consolidated. Perez was the undeniable leader on offense. Per Coach Caniford: "He was a true warrior. Ryan was one of the most competitive kids I've ever coached." For his offensive plan, Caniford decided to make very few changes. "We wanted to do offensively what got us there. We did a pretty good job of spreading it around and letting Perez do his thing. On defense, obviously, we wanted to limit Rodgers as much as possible and take our chances with everybody else. But what made them so scary was that you could shut them down and then boom, they would pop a big play." And that, of course, was most often Rodgers, who could get loose on any given play and gave Lamar that quick score capability. It was how the game ended that became legend in Texas high school football.

Texas State University's Bobcat Stadium is located on the campus of what was at one time Southwest Texas State University. The Bobcats are part of the Sunbelt Conference. San Marcos is located between San Antonio to the South and Austin to the North, but just "up the road" on Interstate 35 from New Braunfels. In fact, many New Braunfels high school students attend Texas State during their senior year, knocking out some early college credits.

The Unicorn faithful made the short drive up to San Marcos and filled the home team side of the stadium. As the stadium filled, I realized that fans were standing along the fenced walkways on each side of the stands. I also became acutely aware of people crowding my own seat on the Lamar side who were wearing the wrong shade of blue. The New Braunfels fans were forced to sit amongst the Mustang crowd. Obviously, the proximity of San Marcos to New Braunfels had turned this into a home field advantage for the Unicorns. Every town in Texas, to some degree or the other, lives vicariously through its high school football team. It is simply more noticeable when they are winning.

The Lamar fans welcomed the Unicorn strays who apologized for being on the wrong side of the stadium. They promised not to be too loud. They just could not stand missing seeing their undefeated Unicorns march on to the state championship game. They assured us they would try to keep their cheering to a minimum. I started wondering how uninformed I was about this New Braunfels team. The vibe from the buzz in the crowd was that Lamar was in for a rude awakening. Another semifinal battle and that old sinking feeling crept in. Had Lamar really blown their best chance at state last year? As per usual the RIOT gang was up front and loud. This was the point where the previous season had ended. The Lamar faithful would do all they could to cheer their boys to the final. But looking across the field at Perez warming up, watching his confident stride and crisp delivery, I couldn't help but remind myself that Lamar had fought hard to get to this point, and this was only going to be harder.

Prior to the game, the players for each team received final instructions from their respective coaches. Nothing new could ever really be introduced at this point in the season. Most of the instructions were reminders of how offenses and defenses would start the first series of play. New Braunfels starting center Ryan Walker had watched film on Consolidated all week and knew what waited for him and his O-line. "We knew they were going to be big, but we still underestimated their size. All week we had watched film on Lamar. Some days we walked out thinking we had it handled. Then the next day we saw them just beat the piss out of good teams and then things were not so rosy. It was like being on a roller coaster. Then on the first series I looked past their big front line, and their linebackers and secondary were just as big. I knew we were in for a real battle."

For the visiting Mustangs, captains Jacquizz Rodgers, DJ Smallwood, Chuck Obi and Sule Osagiede walked out to midfield for the coin toss. From the other side for the New Braunfels Unicorns were captains Jake Johnson, Spencer Jergins, and Josh Knudson. Lamar won the coin toss and elected to defer to the second half. The Unicorns elected to go on offense first. The

Unicorns were the designated home team and were wearing their all royal blue uniforms. Lamar was in their Nike whites with blue numbers outlined in silver. Kicking right to left from the press box view, the Mustang's Adan Gomez boomed the ball down to the New Braunfels 2-yard line where the Unicorns effected a reverse handoff to receiver Travis Steel who brought the ball out to their own 31-yard line. However, a holding penalty against the Unicorns took the ball back to the New Braunfels fifteen. Still, it was a taste of playoff football and things to come for the packed stadium.

Perez opened the game from his usual shotgun formation. After getting nothing on first and second downs, the senior quarterback found his big tight end, Spencer Jergins, on a quick hitter to the New Braunfels 27-yard line for a first down. At 6'4" and 230 pounds, Jergins, who played outside linebacker as his regular position, was often brought in on offense because he was a tough receiver to handle for shorter defensive backs and had great hands. New Braunfels' wide-open offense, under the command of Perez, caused a lot of problems for opponents because of the versatility of so many players. It had been used affectively on their way to thirteen straight wins.

The Unicorn offensive set varied little. On most plays Perez set up in the shotgun with a back on each side. That usually meant Tanner Brown on his right and Justin Garcia on his left. Coach Caniford had kept the same basic game plan throughout the season. They had several different concepts they ran out of that set. Sometimes one back, but usually both of them back there with Perez. According to Caniford: "The play call would depend on how we were blocking it. Sometimes it was actually a called counter play to Perez, while other times it was an outside zone play where Perez could pull it in and run. We also ran a bit of power and power keep." They tried to make a lot of what they were doing look the same but with different blocking schemes. It was predicated upon how accurately Perez read the defense and if the defense overloaded the box or laid back.

Perez had become very comfortable operating Caniford's offense after two years in the system. "Most of it was easy enough to be a pre-snap read, but once the ball was snapped, I had my eye on those certain defenders and made the read based on if they crashed down hard or dropped back. I would say seventy to seventy-five percent of the time we were doing this read option style of playing."

On first down, Perez handed off to Brown who darted through the left side of the offensive line and managed to get to the Unicorn 35-yard line.

On second and two, Perez again set up with an empty backfield. He had Steel running a sideline route to his right and attempted to loft a pass over the defense to the streaking receiver. However, linebacker Carlos Becerra was watching Perez's eyes and quickly dropped back into coverage to make a leaping interception at the forty. He returned it to the New Braunfels 35-yard line for the first turnover of the game.

The Mustang offense took the field and went into their typical I formation with Smallwood under center, Julius Smith behind him in the fullback position, and Jacquizz Rodgers in the running back spot. Staring the Mustangs down from across the line of scrimmage was a stingy Unicorn defense led by surprise phenom linebacker Tom Wort. Wort was somewhat of an oddity in Texas high school football who had emerged as the leader on defense. This defense had shut down the likes of Pflugerville Connally, Alamo Heights, and Gregory Portland on their way to this semifinal round. Coach Caniford explains:

"Tom and his family were from Great Britain. They moved to the United States when he was in late middle school, and he came to us in the Spring of his sophomore year. He was very raw, having had limited exposure to football, but had great physical skills, was a hard worker, and had a gift for finding the football. He played with more fire than anyone I have ever coached. His motor was always running hot, even in practice. He was really fun to coach because every time he put on a helmet it was a game to him. He raised the level of intensity for everyone around him and he carried that on with him to OU where he was a standout linebacker." Wort earned 1st-team all-state linebacker honors in class 4A for the 2007 season and in Class 5A for 2008.

On first down, Smallwood handed off to Rodgers who ran into a wall of defenders for a one-yard gain. On second down, Rodgers received the ball on a quick pitch and hit the right side of the line slipping through tacklers and weaved his way down to the Unicorn 38-yard line, setting up a third and one. Another pitch from Smallwood and Rodgers burst through the line where he broke two tackles on his way down to the 26-yard line for a first and ten. The Mustangs were obviously not feeling the effects of the previous week's slugfest overtime affair with Austin LBJ.

On first down, Smallwood once again pitched to Rodgers going left, but the Unicorn defense was quick to seal off that side of the field. Suddenly, Rodgers hit the brakes and slashed up the middle to the 14-yard line for another first down. New Braunfels saw why so many defenses had trouble containing the Mustang running attack. Another tite toss followed and Quizz barreled down to the 1-yard line for first and goal. Quizz then took the handoff on first down and followed his center, Alex Rohde, and left guard Beny Bravo into the end zone for the game's first score. The point after was no good, and with 7:44 remaining in the first stanza, the Mustangs were out front early.

NEW BRAUNFELS	0
LAMAR CONSOLIDATED	6

Gomez kicked off again, and this time the junior kicker boomed it through the New Braunfels end zone for a touchback. Perez and company took the field looking to get the big royal blue machine humming. On first down, Perez handed off to Garcia who was met quickly by linebackers Chuck Obi and Cory Green for a short gain to the Unicorn 23-yard line. A false start on the offensive line moved the ball back to the New Braunfels 18-yard line for second and twelve. Perez set up with an empty backfield and attempted a screen pass to the left flat to Brown who had gone in motion out of the backfield. Mustang Chuck Obi, from his rover position, read the play all of the way and almost had the second Lamar interception of the night. The defensive pressure applied by the Mustang front four was having an obvious effect on Perez.

On third and twelve, Perez took the snap from the shotgun and was quickly pressured by the Mustang defensive line, forcing the senior signal caller to duck out of several tackles and take off. Perez managed to get to the Unicorn 31-yard line for a much needed first down. The play showcased Perez's ability to scramble out of trouble and create his own running room. On first down, Perez attempted a quarterback keeper but was met at the line by linebacker Sule Osagiede and defensive linemen Deante Ester and Mason Quintanilla for no gain. A handoff to Garcia ended up nowhere, as Osagiede quickly filled the hole for a vicious tackle.

A false start on the offense moved the ball back to the Unicorn 21-yard line for a third and twenty. The aggressive, swarming Mustang defense was creating havoc early. Perez again faced immediate pressure from defensive ends Ester and Andrew Nwaogwugwu that forced him to make a quick throw to his left to Garcia. Cornerback Andrew Okokhere jumped the route and intercepted the ball at the Unicorn 43-yard line. He was taken down by Garcia after running it back to the 40-yard line. A holding penalty against New Braunfels was declined and the Mustang offense was quickly back in business with good field position in New Braunfels territory.

Perez recalls his early struggles. "I just wasn't getting the time I needed, and I was rushing things. Plus, I think we were playing not to lose, including myself, instead of playing our game like we had been doing all year. Their massive defensive line was a problem for me. Not because of them beating our O-line but because of my height. They had these tall defensive ends who were very quick off the line."

Now it was time for the Unicorn defense to get things going as the game was still in the first quarter and the Mustang offense was having its way. Wort, who would go on to star in Bob Stoops' defense in Norman at the University of Oklahoma, never doubted his defense could figure things out. Still, they had not faced an offense as potent as that of Lamar Consolidated and it was taking some time for the Unicorn defense to settle in.

Starting at the New Braunfels 40-yard line the Mustang offense continued to click. After a couple of runs took the ball to the thirty, Rodgers found pay dirt again. On first and ten Smallwood pitched to Rodgers who, seeing the hole was jammed, stutter stepped to his left and sprinted through the New Braunfels secondary into the end zone for a 30-yard touchdown. Wideout Obi threw a key block downfield to spring Rodgers. Gomez put the PAT through the uprights and suddenly Lamar had an early lead and all of the momentum. With 3:26 still remaining in the first quarter, the Mustangs had raced out of the gate.

NEW BRAUNFELS	0
LAMAR CONSOLIDATED	13

On the sideline, the Unicorn defense was a little stunned. Wort knew his defense needed to settle. "We needed to slow the heck down, get composed. It all was happening so quickly. Honestly, Perez never threw interceptions, so we were having to rush back out quickly, and we were not used to that. The first quarter was happening super quick." Meanwhile, on offense the Unicorns needed to do something to give Perez more time to operate.

As the offense sat on the sideline watching the action, they knew something different needed to happen. The O-line in particular was playing poorly. Walker looked at his teammates and his beleaguered quarterback and knew this was shocking to everybody. "We had taken care of Steele [Cibolo High School] and had all of this confidence afterwards. Now there we were watching our QB throw picks when he had thrown almost none during the year and we knew it was on us. We were getting thrown around like rag dolls. They were just so big and physical. At one point it was as if we knew Rufio [Perez] was going to take the brunt of it, so how could we limit the clean shots? He fought through it, though. The guy was a beast."

Perez decided for himself it was time to change things up. "I always felt like the coaches trusted me and I knew I needed to get out of the pocket more to create more opportunities to throw in open lanes instead of trying to go over their tall defensive line. And also to have opportunities to get out into space and tuck it and run. Whatever it took to move the chains."

Gomez booted the kickoff out of the Unicorn end zone for a touchback to set up New Braunfels at their own 20-yard line. Once again, though, a swarming Mustang defense continued to stuff the run and keep Perez off balance. The Unicorns managed to convert a third and four when Perez found Jergins, who hauled in a pass at the New Braunfels 32-yard line. With Osagiede jamming the line of scrimmage on running plays and blitzing to catch Perez off-guard for losses behind the line of scrimmage, it became obvious that the Unicorns were still looking for answers on offense.

On fourth and three, New Braunfels was forced to punt. The Unicorns were not especially happy to be punting to Rodgers and punted towards the sideline most of the night. The punt landed out of bounds at the Lamar 40-yard line giving the Mustang offense good field position with only seconds left in the first quarter. On first down, Smallwood pitched to Quizz, who was hit immediately by linebacker Ryan Grametbauer at the 35-yard line. Somehow Rodgers shrugged off Grametbauer and made his way up to the Lamar 45-yard line. It was the power version of Rodgers all of the way, and the first quarter came to an end with Lamar seemingly in total control.

As the two teams exchanged sides of the field the New Braunfels defense took a collective breath and decided they needed to get back to the original game plan: stop Jacquizz Rodgers and take their chances with everybody else. On second and five Rodgers received the pitch at his own 39-yard line and was met by the Unicorn defense near the Lamar sideline. Just as he tried to put on the brakes and change directions, he was crushed by the backside pursuit of Jergins from his outside linebacker position for a two-yard loss. On third and seven, Smallwood dumped a short pass to Rodgers who powered to the Lamar 49.5-yard line, setting up a fourth down and needing less than a yard for a first to extend the drive.

However, a false start penalty moved the ball back and Wilson decided to punt instead in order to maintain control of field position. His defense had been stifling thus far, so he figured it was better to put the game back in their hands. Taylor Turner's punt went to the New Braunfels 28-yard line where the Unicorn receiver mishandled the ball. Wort, who had hustled back to block, quickly covered the loose ball to avert disaster for an already struggling Unicorn bunch.

Getting the ball back so quickly to their offense was a small victory for the Unicorn defense. Smallwood felt the change in the third possession. "They added more pressure, and the offense just wasn't clicking all of a sudden. They added more blitzes and were now effectively disguising it." It was not a time to panic though as the Unicorn offense so far had no answers for the swarming boys in white.

Wort was pumped that the Unicorn defense had responded. He also knew they were still in for a long afternoon against the Lamar running attack. "Jacquizz was a great opponent. I knew going into the game we were going to go head-to-head a lot. I remember hitting him and being 'Wow, that guy is solid.' The game plan was to get his ass to the ground. Quizz just had that extra step that I couldn't quite time to get a clean hit on him."

Perez and company set up first and ten at their own 28-yard line and desperately needed to get something going. After netting four yards on a running play, Perez opened things up by hitting receiver John Simmons in the left flat on a receiver screen. Simmons then cut inside the Mustang defenders and rambled down to the 48-yard line before being chased down from behind by Becerra. It was a much-needed big play for the Unicorns. However, after a false start penalty moved the ball back to the New Braunfels 43-yard line, things bogged down. Mistakes would be magnified in this semi-final matchup.

It was a disappointing end to a promising drive. The ensuing punt rolled into the end zone for a touchback, and Lamar Consolidated was back in business at their own 20-yard line. At this juncture, there were serious concerns by the Unicorn faithful. The Houston area team was obviously bigger, faster, and stronger. Now the Unicorn defense would be called upon once again to shut down Lamar and Rodgers to keep their team in the game. Perez stood on the sidelines swinging his throwing arm back and forth. Something was amiss. His center stood next to him with a concerned look. Walker sensed the problem. "I'm pretty sure Rufio had a separated shoulder at that point. I wondered if he could throw another pass. But I never doubted he would try."

Tom Wort might not have known much about American football when his family moved to the United States. He might not have known much about the rich history of high school football in Texas. But one thing he did know was that this game had become his passion and the thirteen wins had been the most fun he had ever had in his life. He saw no reason for all of that to change tonight. It was time to get down and dirty, and Tom was like a rodeo bull in the chute waiting for the horn to sound and the gate to fly open.

On second and ten, the New Braunfels faithful were screaming to exhort their boys in royal blue to get a stop before this game got any more out of hand. Smallwood dropped back to pass but was under heavy pressure. He tried to roll to his left, but there were two Unicorns breathing down his neck already. He spied receiver Travis Riedel at the 45-yard line and managed to get the throw off. Unicorn safety Corey Myrik had been reading the play all the way and stepped in front of Riedel for the interception. Myrik immediately turned downfield and ran to the right side to the Lamar 30-yard line. There he slipped a tackle and cut back to the left side of the field following several of his defensive teammates who were now blockers. Lamar's Jarrod Seahorn ran him down from behind to make the tackle at Lamar's own 18-yard line.

Finally, the Unicorns got the break they had been looking for and Perez quickly led his offense onto the field. After managing five yards on first and second down, Perez tried to find Steel for a completion and first down. His pass went just beyond the receiver's outstretched hands. With fourth and five to go, Coach Caniford knew it was time to put some points on the board. He sent out his sure-footed kicker Aaron Hayduck, who connected from twenty-three yards out to cut into Lamar's lead with 6:24 remaining in the first half.

NEW BRAUNFELS	3
LAMAR CONSOLIDATED	13

For now, the Unicorns took solace in the fact that they had stopped the Mustang offense and also finally got on the scoreboard. The mood on the home sideline was lifted and the fans responded. Hayduck booted the kick-off out of the end zone for a touchback. The Lamar offense set up at their own 20-yard line in the I-formation. As the Unicorn defense found new life behind junior linebackers Wort and Grametbauer, the Mustang offense suddenly went stagnant.

On third and ten, the Lamar offensive line jumped for a false start that took the ball back to the fifteen. Faced with third and fifteen, the Mustangs went back to their main man, Rodgers, on a counter play that fooled no one and Rodgers was pushed out of bounds on the Lamar side at the 25-yard line. Another hold against Lamar was declined and the Mustangs were forced to punt on fourth and five. After gaining seventy-six yards on just nine attempts in the first quarter, Rodgers had suddenly been contained. Turner's punt for the Mustangs sailed down to the Lamar 45-yard line where it was mishandled by New Braunfels and ended up being kicked around and down to the New Braunfels 46-yard line where Mustang corner Okokhere pounced on it. It was an instantaneous momentum killer for the boys in royal blue.

With a lucky break in their pocket, the Lamar offense set up to try and get things going as they had in the first quarter. But the Unicorn defense would not budge and looking at a fourth and twenty, Wilson sent Turner back in to punt. He hoped to pin the Unicorns back deep and get into half-time with this lead. Perez and company started at their own 32-yard line with a first and ten. After two short runs by Perez, New Braunfels was facing a third and four. It was crucial to keep this drive going as there was plenty of time for Lamar to mount another scoring drive on offense.

Perez found a streaking John Simmons open downfield for a big gain to the Lamar 16-yard line. Suddenly the Unicorns were in position to cut into the Mustang's lead yet again before the half. With an empty backfield, Perez took the snap on first down and made it to the Lamar twelve. Time was running out and the Unicorns had to hurry. On second down, New Braunfels was called for holding, and the ball was moved back to the Lamar 22-yard line for second and sixteen. Penalties had been costly for both sides all through the first half. On their respective sidelines, both Wilson and Caniford wondered what had happened to the team discipline they had so depended upon.

On the next play, things continued to unravel for New Braunfels as Perez was first hit by a rushing Deante Ester, and then pulled down by Nwaogwugwu at the 37-yard line. This put the Unicorns into a third and twenty-two with time running out. Now it was imperative that Perez either got a score or, at a minimum, put his team in better position to kick a field goal. He fired a bullet down to the Lamar 12-yard line where the pass was hauled in by a wide-open Steel who then slipped two tackles before being hauled down at the 7-yard line. Having used all of his timeouts Caniford was forced to send in his kicker with the clock ticking. Hayduck nailed it from twenty-two yards out, and New Braunfels inched a little closer with only twenty-one seconds left in the first half. An announcement came from the booth that Aledo was leading Copperas Cove 7-0 in their semifinal matchup.

NEW BRAUNFELS	6
LAMAR CONSOLIDATED	13

After a touchback, Lamar coach Wilson elected to have his quarterback take a knee. As the two teams headed to the locker rooms, there were several issues to consider. While New Braunfels had found a way to stop Rodgers and company, they still had not managed to put the ball in the end zone themselves. Perez had two interceptions and the Unicorns lost a fumble on a punt. The mistakes could have been more costly, but this was not the kind of football New Braunfels was used to playing.

On the other side, the Mustang offense got out of the gate quickly but then stalled out in the second quarter. Rodgers managed only six yards rushing on six attempts in that second stanza. Smallwood had a costly interception at a moment when Lamar could have upped the pressure on the Unicorns by adding a third score. The Mustangs also had a missed extra point which tended to be more of a concern during playoff time. While the Mustang defense had managed to keep Perez and his offense out of the end zone, the Unicorns had shown the ability to move the ball in the second quarter. Being down only one score was a victory in and of itself. The two head coaches had some work to do at halftime. This one was far from over.

In the respective locker rooms, the atmosphere was one of relative calm. Neither coaching staff saw reason to panic. For Coach Caniford it was a relief to see his guys battle back after a miserable first quarter. "We played one of our worst quarters of football in the first quarter. We actually felt pretty good at halftime, knowing that we had turned the ball over several times and were only down one score. We just had to execute better and continue to swarm to the football on defense. We knew we had to get as many people to Rodgers as possible, because he was rarely brought down by one tackler. That made us vulnerable to their other playmakers, but we felt we had to slow him down to have a chance, and to do that you had to take some chances."

In the Mustang locker room, it was more of the same. Coach Wilson's opinion was if Lamar was ahead or close at the end of the game it was always their advantage. The Lamar defense needed to dictate the game to Perez, and the offense needed to get Quizz out in space. Offensive coordinator Pat Matthews remembers talking up his guys. "We just needed to get back on track. Our guys jumped out to a quick lead and let their sense of urgency and level of intensity slide. Then New Braunfels did a good job of getting their offense going." One had to wonder if Lamar would come to regret not taking advantage of so many missed opportunities in the first half.

The Mustangs received the second half kick, which Hayduck sent to the back of the end zone for a touchback. A pitch to Quizz on first down netted zero yards. The roar from the opposite stands grew louder than it had all night. On second down, Smallwood executed the tite toss to Rodgers who spurted through the middle for a fourteen-yard gain, but a holding penalty moved the ball back ten yards for a second and twenty. Another quick pitch to Rodgers would net four yards leaving the Mustangs with third and sixteen. The roar of "DEFENSE" began to rise from the overcrowded New Braunfels side of the stadium. They needed their team to come out of halftime and quickly take the momentum. Another tite toss to Quizz netted four more yards, and on third down Smallwood was taken down by Wort at the 18-yard line. This brought the Lamar punting team onto the field.

The start of the second half had a completely different feel compared to the start of the game. New Braunfels was suddenly brimming with confidence and looked like the team that had come into the contest undefeated and on a roll. Turner's punt sailed to the New Braunfels 47-yard line where a fair catch put the Unicorn offense in business with the crowd roaring their approval. From the shotgun Perez took the snap, faked to Castilleja, and was swallowed up by Ward and Nwaogwugwu for a two-yard loss. This Mustang defense prided themselves on being a second half unit, and nothing was going to change that.

On third and ten, Perez was forced to throw early due to the bull rush of Nwaogwugwu. The pass sailed over the head of the intended receiver, but the referee called a roughing the passer penalty on Lamar, which gave the Unicorns a fresh set of downs at the Lamar 37-yard line. Yet another inexcusable mistake. On second and eight, Perez ran up the middle to the Lamar 35-yard line where he was hit hard. He kept his feet and bounced it outside. He was finally pushed out of bounds on the New Braunfels sideline by Okokhere at the 15-yard line. The senior gunslinger had gotten his reads down and took advantage of the swarming, but sometimes over-pursuing, Mustang defense.

After a timeout to collect himself, Perez found Steel for five yards down to the Lamar ten. A big third and five had Perez tucking and running down to the 5-yard line where he was met by free safety Steven Fleming. It set up first and goal for a Unicorn offense that had found its stride. Meanwhile it was announced that Copperas Cove was now leading Aledo 15-9 in their semifinal matchup. After two rushing attempts by Perez took the ball down to the Mustang goal line, the quarterback leapt over the pile on third to score New Braunfels' first touchdown of the contest. Hayduck nailed the extra point and, with 4:28 remaining in the third quarter, the game was suddenly all tied up.

NEW BRAUNFELS	13
LAMAR CONSOLIDATED	13

It was now up to the Mustang offense to get things going. Rodgers had been effective when in space in the opening stanza. But the Unicorns had shut things down since then and seemed to now have all of the momentum. The roar from the home team side filled the stadium and the royal blue fans were on their feet, sensing their boys were on a roll. Hayduck's kick sailed out of the back of the North end zone. The Unicorn faithful remained on their feet, and the roar of "Defense" was deafening as Smallwood went into shotgun formation on first down. Smallwood was dropped back at the 14-yard line and now the New Braunfels fans were in a frenzy. The blood was in the water and the sharks were circling.

On second and fourteen, Rodgers took the handoff and gashed through the right guard-tackle hole made by Paul Alford and Presley Godson. He dragged several Unicorn defenders to the 26-yard line leaving Lamar with a third and four. Another quick hitter by Rodgers to the 31-yard line was nullified by a holding penalty that took the ball back to the 16-yard line. The Mustangs needed a big play to dig themselves out of this hole. On third and long, Wilson called a screen to Quizz, but Grametbauer sniffed it out quickly and dropped the running back at the Lamar 12-yard line. The possession had been a disaster and had kept the Unicorns in the driver's seat late in the third quarter.

Turner's punt rolled out of bounds on the Mustang sideline at the Lamar 47-yard line. Perez and company quickly took the field looking for their first lead. From the shotgun, Perez took the snap and faked a handoff. Castilleja had slipped out of the backfield to Perez's left. Perez stopped suddenly and turned to throw a backwards pass for the screen to Castilleja who lost sight of the ball at the last second. The pass bounced off the running back and hit the turf where it was quickly pounced on by the Mustangs' Becerra, who thought the pass was possibly a backwards lateral. The officials agreed and gave possession to the Mustangs, who were back in business at the Unicorns' 48-yard line. Becerra credits his coaching for the turnover. "It was fifty-fifty whether the pass was backwards or not, but we were always coached when the ball is on the ground you jump on it. The refs had not blown the whistle, so I figured it was a live ball."

Wilson wasted no time in going to his bread and butter. On first down, Smallwood handed to Rodgers, who slipped quickly beyond the line of scrimmage and darted down to the 41-yard line. On third and two, a tite toss to Rodgers took the ball down to the 36-yard line for another first down. The third quarter came to an end with Lamar at the New Braunfels' thirty-two.

As the two teams exchanged sides of the field, the Mustangs decided to put the game in Rodgers hands and take their chances. A squad that prided itself on being a second half team was ready to turn the momentum back in their favor. On the other side was a New Braunfels squad that had evened things up and felt their destiny was back in their own hands as long as they continued to play Unicorn football. The first order of business for their defense was to shut down Rodgers who was trying to catch fire in this second half, as was his style.

On second and six, Smallwood set up in the shotgun with Rodgers as the lone back. An inside fake to Rodgers drew in the entire Unicorn defensive line. Smallwood quickly scampered outside towards the right flat where he got a key block by wide receiver Travis Riedel. This allowed him to get all the way to the Unicorn eighteen before being pushed out of bounds by Chris Taha. It was the dilemma that all defenses faced when taking on Lamar. You could load the box and stop Quizz, but it made it very hard to account for a very athletic quarterback who could kill you with his legs or his arm. On the sidelines, Coach Caniford shook his head, as this type of play made for a long night.

"That was what made them so scary," remembers Caniford. "You could stop them on multiple plays in a row, but they had the ability to pop a big one." On first and ten Wilson stayed with the shotgun-one back set. An inside handoff to Rodgers took the ball down to the fourteen. The same play on second down had Rodgers carrying down to the 7-yard line for a first and goal. New Braunfels was quickly being reminded why Jacquizz Rodgers was the best running back, if not player, in class 4A that year. He had owned the fourth quarter all year. Rodgers took the handoff on first down and immediately faced a blitzing Taha. Rodgers quickly put on the brakes and cut inside. He then powered through several more Unicorn defenders on his way into the end zone. Gomez hit the extra point to cap off a huge series for the Mustangs. The drive was vintage Lamar and suddenly put the Unicorns back on their heels again. With 10:57 left in the fourth quarter this contest had swung back in Lamar's favor.

| NEW BRAUNFELS | 13 |
| LAMAR CONSOLIDATED | 20 |

After the touchback, the Unicorns set up first and ten at their own twenty. On first down, defensive end Ester blew through his block and took Perez down for a three-yard loss. Suddenly it was the Mustang defenders who were strutting their stuff after being quiet for two quarters. Ester again put heavy pressure on the Unicorn quarterback, forcing him to overthrow his receiver on second down. Looking at third and thirteen, Perez stood in the shotgun and knew he needed a big play. Castilleja went in motion out of the backfield, leaving Perez with an empty set. That gave Perez his own favorite play, the power option. This run-read option was created for guys like Perez who thrived on reading defenses and making them pay once they showed their hand.

Perez took the snap and fired a perfect strike to a wide-open Travis Steel at the New Braunfels 32-yard line. Steel was finally tackled at the thirty-six by defensive back Okokhere. Perez then kept for five yards on first down, showing his uncanny ability to slip in and out of tackles. At 5' 10" and 170 lbs., Perez was not an overpowering runner. His ability to get into lanes and avoid tackles was the thing that made him so effective. And he never gave up on a run, much like Rodgers. On second down, Perez eluded a blitzing Osagiede and carried the ball to the New Braunfels 48-yard line for another first down. With plenty of time on the clock the Unicorn offense was methodically moving down the field.

After a short run by Garcia, Perez once again found Steel for a gain to the Lamar 40-yard line. The Mustang defense was having trouble matching up on the wide-open sets thrown at them by Caniford while trying to keep tabs on Perez. On second down, Perez found Greg Laird open at the 31-yard line and hit him between the numbers. Laird escaped the first tackle before being hit by Fleming at the twenty. He managed to keep his feet and continued all the way down to the Lamar fifteen where defensive back Quentin Palmer finally stopped him. Caniford's play calling along with Perez's decision making were spot on. On first down, Nwaogwugwu dragged Perez down back at the 20-yard line for a loss and momentarily slowed the Unicorn assault.

Perez got six of it back on the next play, leaving New Braunfels with a third and nine. Nwaogwugwu once again came crashing down on Perez on third down, which forced the ball to be under thrown to Castilleja in the right flat. Now the Unicorns were left with a huge fourth down. The big, athletic Mustang defensive line had reasserted itself and the Mustangs were making a stand. Perez needed a big play once again on this all important potentially game tying drive. On fourth down, Perez faced a blitzing Osagiede who had a direct bead on him. The suddenness of the rush forced Perez to throw quickly, and he was intercepted in the end zone by Okokhere, who ran it out to the Lamar 7-yard line. New Braunfels was called for holding which Lamar declined. The air was let out of the Unicorn sideline.

Now it was up to the Mustang offense to get some first downs and run the clock. The New Braunfels defense was left with the unenviable task of stopping the potent running attack of Lamar while saving as many precious seconds as they possibly could. The Mustangs managed only a single yard on runs by Quizz on first and second down. The resolve of the Unicorn defense was obvious. On third down, Smallwood misfired a pass to his receiver and the punt team came on.

The fired-up Unicorn defense had done exactly what they needed by holding Lamar to three and out. Turner set up deep in his own end zone for the punt. He got off a booming punt to Steel waiting at the fifty. However, Steel misjudged the ball and ducked out at the last second. The ball hit at the Lamar 48-yard line and rolled all the way down to the thirty-three where it was downed by Palmer. The mistake was costly because there now were less than three minutes remaining in the game and every yard counted.

The Unicorn offense took the field knowing this could be their last chance to extend the season. They knew they could move the ball, but they had to score a touchdown. A field goal did them no good at this stage of the game. They started the drive with three short passes up to their own 43-yard line, where on first and ten Perez found Castilleja for a strike into Lamar territory at the thirty-four. The Unicorns were now going no huddle as time ticked off the clock.

Perez tried two quick runs and managed to get another first down at the Lamar 21-yard line. On first and ten he found Jergins running a slant across the middle. Initially it looked like Jergins had room to run, but rover Chuck Obi flashed in quickly for a diving tackle, taking Jergins' feet out from under him at the Mustang fifteen. Next, Perez kept for a grinding run down to the Lamar eight for a first and goal. However, on first down Perez was flushed out of the pocket and taken down near the New Braunfels sideline by Nwaogwugwu for a fifteen-yard loss. Perez jumped up in disgust as the Unicorns were forced to use a precious timeout. On second down, Perez attempted a short pass that was broken up by a vicious hit from Becerra on the intended receiver. New Braunfels had to call its last timeout.

It was now third and goal from the Lamar 21-yard line. The Unicorns had time enough for one, maybe two more plays. Perez set up in the shotgun with an empty backfield. At this point the Lamar defenders were jumping up and down trying to get the Mustang faithful on their feet to make some noise. Ester remembers defensive team captain Osagiede telling the secondary to get ready on the side of Jergins who tended to be their big target when they needed a play. "During the timeout, the coaches were telling us that New Braunfels had to throw it into the end zone. We knew who they were going to. We told Quentin to get ready, they were throwing his way. It was predictable at that stage of the game. And we knew Perez could extend plays, so we told everybody to stay disciplined, to stay focused."

The Unicorns set up in the shotgun with an empty backfield. Everybody was in the pattern. Perez pump faked and then waited until the last second to launch a perfect strike into the back of the end zone on the right side into the waiting hands of Spencer Jergins. The gunslinger in royal blue had one more miracle in his back pocket and the Unicorns needed only an extra point to send this crazy game into overtime. Aaron Hayduck calmly stepped onto the playing field and split the uprights to tie it all up with just fourteen seconds on the game clock.

| NEW BRAUNFELS | 20 |
| LAMAR CONSOLIDATED | 20 |

The New Braunfels faithful were deafening as they roared their approval. On the Lamar sideline, things had gotten a little tense as tempers flared. Palmer was beside himself. "Emotions were through the roof. I thought I had possibly just ruined our season. Sule and I had a very heated exchange, and it wasn't pretty. We had never lost our cool like that, but it was understandable. All I could think about was how I could redeem myself."

Ester felt the frustration as well. "I remember yelling at Quentin... how the hell could you let that happen? After a few minutes we cooled down. The thing is... we never thought anybody was actually going to beat us. But Perez was frustrating. We had rode him hard all night and he just kept getting up and coming right back at us. I don't think too many quarterbacks could take what he did and then come back like that. We had never faced anyone like him."

New Braunfels tried a surprise pooch kick that was recovered at the Lamar forty-five by a quick-thinking Jose Pena. On first down Wilson called his special play for this game "Unicorn." The Mustangs set up in a one back set and Smallwood sent Quizz in motion from the backfield. The play was designed to get Rodgers out into the pattern in the right flat while tight end Dominique Briggs was the actual target down the middle. Quizz would then turn up the sideline as the second read for Smallwood. Wilson called the pattern a "wide go from the backfield." Smallwood got flushed out of the pocket and took off for the Lamar sideline where he was pushed out at the New Braunfels forty-five. However, a holding penalty against Lamar placed the ball back to the Mustang 42-yard line. The Mustangs set up with four receivers to the right and Smallwood in the shotgun. The junior quarterback launched down to the Unicorn 10-yard line where the ball was knocked down and regulation ended with the score tied.

It was hard to imagine that after going into overtime the previous week Lamar would find itself in the exact same situation just one week later. Yet, here they were, watching the momentum shift back and forth until the whole thing ended right back where it started. There was no time to reflect. The coaches went out for the coin toss and New Braunfels went on offense first, setting up at the Lamar 25-yard line. Each team would have a chance in overtime. Caniford went right back to his game plan with no hesitation. He put the ball in Perez's hands and let his senior do his thing. On first down Perez kept and zig-zagged his way down to the Lamar sixteen for a nifty nine-yard gain.

On second down, Perez pump faked and then followed his fullback Tanner Brown up the middle for another seven yards to the nine and a first and goal. It was textbook Unicorn football all of the way with Perez reading the defense and trusting his offensive line to get him into space. A quick handoff to Castilleja netted two yards. On second and goal, Perez took the snap and attempted to roll to his left, but linebacker Osagiede had shot the gap and was immediately in the quarterback's face. Perez still attempted to get the pass off but threw into the waiting arms of free safety Fleming in the end zone. Fleming attempted to run the ball out but was taken out on the New Braunfels sideline by Perez himself, who then crumpled to the turf. Fleming got up holding his right wrist. Perez was prostrate on the sideline, completely gassed. The persistent defensive pressure of the Lamar front four and the athleticism of Osagiede had shone bright yet again. It was another unfortunate turnover for New Braunfels. This now left the Mustangs in the driver's seat, needing only a field goal to seal the win.

Smallwood set up shop at the twenty-five from the shotgun with Rodgers to his right. It did not take a stretch of the imagination to know what Coach Wilson was thinking at this moment. "We always expected to score. We would never get away from our power game. At the minimum either Jacquizz would score or get us into chip shot field goal range." On first down, Quizz took the handoff and ran straight into Tom Wort for no gain. Smallwood faked to Rodgers on second and sliced his way down to the 18 1/2-yard line leaving the Mustangs with a short third and three. A quick give to Quizz on third down netted zero yards as Wort and Grametbauer jammed the middle to close the hole. Still, the Mustangs were in great shape and kicker Gomez had already proven he could perform under pressure.

As the junior kicker counted his steps back, Becerra kneeled down ready to take the snap. Suddenly Caniford called a timeout to ice the Mustang kicker. With eight men on the line and three back in case of a fake, the Unicorns prepared for one last desperate effort to remain alive. The snap was good, and Gomez stepped into his kick. However, Wort, who had lined up to the left side of the offensive line managed to spurt through an opening. Unblocked, he got a hand on the ball which sent it backwards. A Unicorn defender picked the ball up but was tackled at the thirty as a jubilant Wort raced across midfield pumping his arms and throwing his head back and forth wildly. The defensive heart and soul of the boys in royal blue had come up big one more time and this game was headed to a second overtime. The New Braunfels fans came off life support one more time in a roaring crescendo of support.

The two teams walked to the south end of the field to start the second overtime, still locked in a 20-20 dead heat. This time it would be the Mustangs who would go on offense first. Wilson put his offense in its traditional power I formation with fullback Julius Smith in a three-point stance in front of Rodgers and Smallwood under center. There would be no more trick plays. It was time for smash-mouth football and a big dose of Jacquizz Rodgers. A tite toss to Rodgers on first down saw the Mustang running back power down to the nineteen for second and four. After gaining only a yard on second down the Mustangs came to the line for a third and three. From the shotgun Smallwood handed the ball to Rodgers on a small delay and Rodgers scooted around the left side behind a wall created by the blocking of Pena and Bravo. He followed his pulling big man Godson who crushed the right defensive end of the Unicorns. This allowed Rodgers to escape outside where he split the two Unicorn defensive backs and glided into the end zone for a touchdown. A Gomez extra point attempt was good, and just like that Lamar was back on top.

| NEW BRAUNFELS | 20 |
| LAMAR CONSOLIDATED | 27 |

Somehow an exhausted Ryan Perez brought his troops back out for one more offensive set. The senior signal caller would do everything humanly possible to keep his Unicorns alive and breathing. Keeping on first and second downs, Perez got the Unicorns down to the Lamar fifteen for a fresh set of downs. Caniford continued to call # 4's number and Perez kept on gashing until he finally got to a first down and goal at the Lamar three-yard line. Twice he crashed into the middle of the line only to come up just short. Finally, on third and one he slipped under the diving tackle of Obi to hit pay dirt for the touchdown and gave the Unicorns one more chance to tie things up. Hayduck split the uprights and the two teams were headed for a third overtime.

NEW BRAUNFELS	27
LAMAR CONSOLIDATED	**27**

Once more the teams switched end zones with the New Braunfels offense setting up at the 25-yard line. Perez operated from the shotgun with an empty set. Garcia, who was split out to Perez's left went in motion to the right. Perez took the snap and flipped the ball to Garcia in front of him. Meanwhile, receiver Steel, who had split out right, came back across the field to his left. Garcia flipped the ball to Steel who then flipped it back to Perez for the flea flicker. The pass thrown to the right side of the end zone fell incomplete. Caniford was looking to shake things up and possibly get some pressure off of his battered quarterback.

Perez went right back on second down and hit his big guy Jergins on the slant inside for a gain to the sixteen that left them with a third and short. Perez then kept down to the twelve for a gain of three and a new set of downs. Castilleja took it on first down to the ten where he was stopped by Ward, leaving the Unicorns with a second and five. With trips right, including Jergins in the slot, Perez took the snap in the shotgun but pump faked and ran to the 8-yard line. On third down and six, Perez fired to Steel in the right side of the end zone, but Palmer was there to knock the pass down. The Mustang cornerback had finally gotten the chance to redeem himself and left the Unicorns with a field goal opportunity to take the lead. Hayduck came on to try a kick from the right hash mark to put his team up by three. With Palmer and Rodgers flying in from each side the kicker some-how managed to push it just a bit to the left and the field goal was no good.

The Consolidated Mustangs set up at the 25-yard line, knowing they just needed to get a field goal in this third overtime to end the contest. However, Coach Wilson was not thinking play it safe. "We never thought about just trying to get it to field goal range. We felt like we needed to just go for the score because kicking had become anything but a sure thing in this game." On first down, Smallwood handed off to Rodgers who crashed into the line for a short two-yard gain. On second and eight, Smallwood set up in the shotgun with Rodgers to his right. He gave to Quizz who tried to get out-side to his left but again was met by a host of Unicorns and managed to get back only to the line of scrimmage. However, a holding penalty against the Mustangs moved the ball back to the 34-yard line. This was not the type of series Wilson and his offense needed at this time of the night. New Braunfels had just missed a field goal and the Mustangs were given a chance to end this grueling contest. Now here they were going backwards and somewhat effectively taking themselves out of their power running game.

THE CATCH PART II

Smallwood brought his offense to the line and started calling the sig-nals. The play call was to try "Unicorn" again. It had not worked earlier in the game and had gone so badly that New Braunfels would still not expect it. "Unicorn" called for a one back set with Quizz exiting to his right on the aforementioned wide go from the backfield. On a wide go, the running back will run towards the sideline to receive a pass on a flare route out in the flat but also can then suddenly turn upfield at the sideline. What made this particular play different was the snap from center.

Smallwood surveyed the coverage from the shotgun, first right and then left. He licked his fingers and prepared to call the cadence when suddenly center Alex Rohde launched a low spiral that veered slightly to Smallwood's right side. The ball skipped just behind the feet of right guard Presley God-son but close enough that Smallwood scooped it up while keeping his eyes on the oncoming Unicorn rush. The second miracle was that Travis Riedel, who had lined up as the wide receiver to the right side, almost booted the ball when he had come in motion to his left. He had just barely crossed the point of the center in front of Smallwood when the snap occurred. Somehow the snap missed Riedel's legs. Riedel recalls how it went down. "I wasn't supposed to go in motion, but DJ gave me the leg pat. What that ended up doing was cause the New Braunfels DB to go with me, freeing up Quizz for more of a one-on-one coverage." The momentum of retrieving the ball took Smallwood several steps to the right side of the quickly collapsing pocket. Right tackle Paul Alford was quick to pick up the rushing Unicorn defensive end and pushed him to the outside of the pocket to his right.

However, Smallwood's momentum in retrieving the snap had taken him further out to the right than would normally be expected, so Alford had blocked his guy right into Smallwood. Seeing what was happening, Smallwood put on the brakes and stepped back left inside of Alford's block, which had now put the Unicorn defender on the ground, thus buying himself time to regain his footing and survey the field.

New Braunfels' Jergins had come in from the other side and was quickly bearing down on Smallwood, who had regained his footing and prepared to throw. Just as Jergins launched himself and his outstretched arms at Smallwood, the junior signal caller with the big arm launched a rocket to the right side of the end zone.

Meanwhile, Rodgers seeing all of this happening, felt the cornerback on his side break back towards the line of scrimmage so he turned upfield. Quizz knew exactly what to do on the broken play. "I felt the corner break up, so I took it deep." He looked back and saw his quarterback setting his feet for the throw and knew the ball was coming his way. Smallwood knew he had to get the ball thirty-three yards into the end zone but drop it in just over the two Unicorn defenders who were now frantically trying to get back into coverage. Smallwood cocked his arm and "dropped a dime" in football parlance. Rodgers never broke stride as he hauled in the pass near the back end of the right side of the end zone.

Quizz's momentum carried him onto the outside of the track that surrounded the San Marcos field. He turned to look back and saw no yellow flags. Game over. Walk off touchdown. Rodgers heaved the ball into the air as his teammates ran to congratulate him. Tight end Dominique Briggs was the first one to reach Rodgers, yelling, "That's what I'm talking about."

The Unicorn defenders could only wonder as they tried to process the play that had just happened. Their head coach, Chuck Caniford, summarized it best. "It was a busted play. When the snap was fumbled, our eyes came off of our keys and they made a play. It seemed like one of those plays where if they had executed it without the muffed snap, it may not have been as successful. But that one brief second where the defense sees the ball on the ground is enough to get that pause, and then you realize the play is alive and now you have lost Rodgers. Still, that was a helluva recovery, helluva pass, and you knew Rodgers was going to make that catch."

Tackle Jose Pena remembers the exhilaration of the big win. "I don't recall being tired or even thinking about the fact that we had just played three overtime periods. All I knew was we were actually going to state. It wasn't until we were on the bus after eating that we came down from that high. Of course, the next day my whole body ached."

Perez, for his part, had left it all out on the field. Still, the senior quarterback had led his team to a perfect season until this night. He was inconsolable on the sideline and felt responsible personally for the loss. "After the game was over, I blamed myself. I thought about what I could have done better to give us an opportunity to win the game."

Nothing could have been further from the truth. Had it not been for Perez's tenacity and character the Unicorns would have wilted early on after the Mustangs roared out of the gates and the defense collected a couple of interceptions. His coach was well aware of the heroic effort he received from his star signal caller. Caniford was very proud. "Rufio (Perez) was such a fierce competitor and a tremendous leader, so it didn't surprise me that he carried the weight of that game on his shoulders. But anyone who saw that game knows that he had no reason to hang his head. He was a true warrior on that field. Most guys would have folded after the first quarter, but he just kept fighting and his teammates responded to that. That was the most electric atmosphere I've ever been a part of, and I still have people want to talk about that game. We were all so proud of our guys and the heart that they showed that night and our fans were amazing. That game was a great example of what Friday night football in Texas is all about."

Unicorn center Walker saw his quarterback on the sideline and understood the pain. "Seeing Rufio laid out, totally exhausted, trying to shoulder the blame for the loss was heartbreaking. We wouldn't have even been in the game if it hadn't been for him. He took a great team to three overtimes. Truth is… nobody deserves to lose a game like that… nobody."

The Lamar Consolidated Mustangs of 2007 had now done what the preceding team had been incapable of doing. They had punched their ticket to the school's first ever trip to the Texas state football championship. It had taken an overtime victory against Austin LBJ at Kyle Field and a triple overtime victory against an undefeated New Braunfels team in San Marcos. Yet, here they were, just one win away from winning it all. They were going to state. The only negative that night on the bus going home was the news that first team All-state free safety Steven Fleming's injured wrist was a fracture. The junior interceptions leader would not be suiting up for the school's biggest game in its history. His backup? Jacquizz Rodgers.

For the night Rodgers, rushed for 158 yards on thirty-two carries becoming only the seventh player in Texas high school football history to eclipse 8000 yards rushing. Rodgers last touchdown would bring his total to 133. He entered the contest tied with Cuero's Robert Strait. Rodgers quickly broke that record in the first quarter. He ended the night with five total touchdowns. He would now head into the state final looking to extend his new touchdown record against a tough Copperas Cove Bulldawgs team who would be making their second appearance in the state final after closing out a tough Aledo team 15-9. Cove was led by senior quarterback Robert Griffin III and junior first team all-state linebacker Tanner Brock. The title game would take place the following Saturday in Round Rock in the same stadium in which the Mustangs' previous season had ended.

Years later, Caniford would reflect. "It was clear to me that both teams had tremendous leadership, and that gets overshadowed by the individual stars who were on the field that night. Those kids were obviously special players, but to this day, that team was the most committed team with the best leadership that I've ever coached. Our offensive line set the tone every day in practice, and we had a tremendous senior class that was committed to achieving their goals and were very selfless players."

Brandon C. Williams: Quizz, Brandon Williams, Chronicle. Tell me about the touchdown catch.

Jacquizz Rodgers: Oh man, I was just trying to make a big play and I did that. Everyone thought we were going to lose. We came through one more time and played hard through those last seconds."

Brandon C. Williams: Darrell, tell me about the play.

Darrell Smallwood: To tell you the truth, the play was busted, it wasn't designed to go that way. I just had to get the ball and refocus myself. Get set again. I saw Quizz in the end zone. I knew I could make that pass. That's how we practice. Stay focused in practice and that determines how we play. You stay focused in practice and big plays like that will always happen.

Next up, State.

CHAPTER 12

STATE

Copperas Cove Bulldawgs

The morning of December 15, 2007 marked the fifth Saturday in a row the Lamar training staff was up early getting things done at Traylor Stadium. A playoff checklist had to be knocked out before the players arrived. Gear had to be loaded on the buses. Supplies, med kits, and such had to be stocked, restocked, and then checked again. Once that bus pulled out, Lance Hale and Dennis Fyke would not have the luxury of forgetting something. And this was State.

In his office, head coach Lydell Wilson sat at his desk, thinking mostly about the logistics of the day ahead. But somewhere, way back there in the depths of dreaming, he knew he had his team on the precipice of the school's first ever state championship in football. This school, the one he and his late brother starred at. The one he always related to on the deepest level. A school in a town he grew up in, where his "people" lived and raised sons. Sons he now depended on to execute his grand plan. He would be judged by this day for the rest of his life.

A coach can go through his or her entire career and never have a moment like that. All of the work and sacrifice and planning doesn't guarantee there will be moments of glory. Now here he was, just like last year, so close to seeing that goal fulfilled, but not knowing exactly how it would all unfold. Wilson couldn't help but wonder. What had not been done? What stone was left unturned? Would Quizz do his thing? Would DJ react better than the previous year when he was a sophomore against Alamo Heights? Would the defense, tasked with dealing with Robert Griffin, come through as brilliantly as they had thus far? Too many questions for this morning. Better to keep thinking about buses, and meals, and the drive ahead. All that could have been done was done. It was up to the kids now.

The buses pulled out onto Avenue I in Rosenberg from the back of the high school before noon. The players and coaches were loaded up with their iPods and headphones, listening to music and trying to relax. Wilson had decided to take a different approach to game day. "I didn't want us sitting around all day waiting to do something. So instead of driving up the night before, we left late Saturday morning."

The players filled the back of the buses and the coaches sat up front. At this point there really was not anymore coaching left to do. This bus ride was going to be about relaxing and reflecting. OC Matthews settled quickly into his seat and got comfortable. He had every intention of getting a good long nap. A very long, intense night lied ahead. Although he could hear the soft murmur from the back of the bus, the rumble of the big bus engine would take care of any threat of insomnia. The coordinator was in snooze land before the bus turned up Highway 36 headed west.

Out in San Francisco, All-Pro safety Michael Lewis was preparing for the 49ers' Sunday contest. There were still fine details to iron out, and Lewis, like most professional athletes, had his typical pregame routine to adhere to. But he also had that extra little something to occupy his mind this weekend. His protege, a very special nephew, was playing in a very special game. The significance of that opportunity did not escape Uncle Mike. Lewis was from Texas, and he knew full-well all that there was to know about Texas high school football and the doors that could be opened by excellence in the sport.

"I told Quizz that he had a chance to make history. I reminded him that all of their names would have 'State' written behind them, and coming from a small town like Richmond or Rosenberg, that would be special. I told him that you play the game of football to be called a champion, and that he and his teammates could relive those moments forever, and that bond could never be taken away. Mostly, I told my nephew to live in the moment and take advantage of this golden opportunity. Go take it!"

Older brother James Rodgers was up in Corvallis, sitting in his dorm room waiting for updates. Still basking in the huge win over state rival Oregon, James could not help but feel like good things were happening for the Rodgers family. As much as he would had loved to of been in Round Rock, business was business and he needed to be away. The brothers always talked after games, so it had been a few days since he had spoken to Quizz. But he knew exactly where his younger sibling's mind was... totally focused on finishing unfinished business. The plan was very much intact.

Likewise, Uncle Rodney Williams was preparing himself mentally and emotionally for the day that was ahead. Rodney and Quizz's mother Tasha traveled to the game together. Rodney acknowledged the long odds going into the title game. "We all knew about RG III and the state quality track squad they called a football team. There was plenty to worry about. Plus, they had already been to the finals, there wouldn't be any stage fright on their part. But... I always said bet on Quizz."

Driving up to Round Rock felt like returning to the scene of the crime. The Mustangs did not fare well here the previous season in their semifinal loss to Alamo Heights. My last memory of Kelly Reeves Athletic Complex was that of the Mustangs having their hearts ripped out by a surging Mules team that went on to defeat Copperas Cove for their first ever state title. As the caravan neared Bastrop, the team stopped at the state park for lunch. Scarfing down some sub sandwiches was yet another chance to break up the monotony of waiting for kickoff.

Why Round Rock? Why couldn't it have been anywhere else?

On top of everything else, a cold front had blown in. The winter storm started somewhere probably in Montana, traveled down through Wyoming, surged as it passed through the Rockies such that by the time it hit the feedlots of Dalhart and Dumas in the Texas panhandle, old man winter was giving no quarter. While Copperas Cove may have been used to some winter weather, the boys from the Gulf Coast were not. I wondered how the Lamar guys would react to a near zero wind chill factor. I knew I hated it.

Copperas Cove was in the final for the second consecutive year behind the offensive play of quarterback Robert Griffin III, running backs Troy Vital and Brandin Byrd, and receiver/returner Josh Boyce. On defense they had first team All-State linebacker Tanner Brock, son of defensive coordinator Reb Brock. The Dawgs were a little banged up. Vital had his ankle taped extra tight and the cold was not helping things. The first team all-state running back would give his offense all he could. "I suffered a high ankle sprain the week before against Aledo. It limited me a little, and the cold wasn't helping keep things loose." The injury and Lamar's swarming defense caused the Dawgs' head coach to institute some changes into his offense. Said Vital:

"We knew they would be active and flying to the ball, so we wanted to use that against them with counters and misdirections." Vital was sporting the #11 jersey in honor of his brother Keith Jr. who had been killed.

For Cove head coach Jack Welch, the game plan was simple: "Get first downs and control the clock." He also was aware of Lamar's swarming defense. "We wanted to run the plays that got us to the championship. The change up was that we had not run Robert [Griffin] on much of the counter stuff so we mixed in more of the misdirection guard-tackle plays and let him carry it. We assumed that they knew the misdirection fullback counter had been a staple for us, so we faked it and ran the option off of it with Griffin and Vital."

Robert Lee Griffin III was born on February 12, 1990, in Okinawa, Japan where his parents were stationed in the US Army. Both Robert II and Jacqueline were sergeants. The Griffin family later moved to Tacoma, Washington and then New Orleans, Louisiana before arriving in Copperas Cove in 1997. Copperas Cove is west of Killeen, which is home to Fort Hood in central Texas. His childhood was that of an army brat. Fortunately for Copperas Cove, Fort Hood was his father's base during Griffin's high school years.

Griffin was a three-sport athlete, excelling in track, basketball, and football. Known mostly for his prowess as a quarterback after winning the Heisman Trophy at Baylor, Griffin's greatest achievements in high school were in track. He set state and national records in the 110-meter high hurdles and 400-meter intermediate hurdles. He was ranked number one in the nation in the intermediates. Although he passed his way to stardom as a Baylor Bear, it was his ability to run and create at Copperas Cove that paved the way to back-to-back state championship games. He was senior class president and graduated seventh in his class.

Griffin went on to win the coveted Heisman Trophy presented annually by the New York Downtown Athletic Club, and he was considered a possible number one draft pick in the NFL. Again, as with the Heisman race, it was a toss-up between he and Andrew Luck. Griffin also garnered such accolades as the 2011 Associated Press College Football Player of the Year, and the Davey O'Brien Award as the nation's top quarterback. The Washington Redskins moved up in the 2012 NFL draft and they selected Griffin with the second pick. Griffin, like his counterpart DJ Smallwood from Lamar, went into the 2007 high school football season with unfinished business.

His high school offensive coordinator, Tracy Welch, monitored the young Robert Griffin's progress from the time he was in elementary school. "We started hearing about him early. He was already setting records in track at Williams-Ledger Elementary. The coaches wrote letters to younger players to get them excited about high school football. Robert wrote me as well and he always signed his letters 'Your Future Quarterback.' He continued to set records in track in junior high. We moved him to varsity his sophomore year where he played a little quarterback and some receiver.

"We as coaches hope we had something to do with his development both as an outstanding young man and as a football player. But with Robert, everything starts and finishes with family. His family was both athletic and tight knit. His mom came to practice with a chair, an umbrella, and a video camera. Then they went home and studied Robert's reads, mechanics, everything. He was so focused, so competitive at such an early age. His coach at Baylor, Art Briles, had a saying something like 'no pressure, no diamonds'. We had sayings also, as most teams do. Robert took that stuff to heart."

After his sophomore year in high school, Robert was ready to lead the Bulldawgs. He also continued to excel in track and set records his junior year before going to Baylor early in the Spring of what would have been his senior year in high school. Griffin was known around Cove as a hard worker whose family was dedicated to helping their son be the best at everything he did. Tracy Welch remembers Robert doing things on his own to improve himself athletically. "I was driving home after practice… after practice…. and I saw this car on the shoulder of the road with their hazard lights on. They were at the top of the hill. Robert was in front dragging a tire with a harness and rope. Robert would get to the top of the hill, about a quarter of a mile, and then jump on the back of the car and they would take him back down to the bottom of the hill. He would jump off and run back up that hill dragging the tire."

Griffin was also known to be a perfectionist in all of his trades, especially track. Welch remembers an incident at a track meet that, to this day, still has him shaking his head. "Robert was running the 110-meter hurdles. His goal was always to be crossing the finish line when the second-place runner was clearing the last hurdle, which was most of the time. At this one meet, I went to congratulate him on winning and I could see he was visibly upset. I asked him what was up, and he said one of the hurdles was off in distance. He knew because his steps were perfect, and he had run the hurdles that many times in his life. I checked with the meet officials, and they remeasured. The hurdle that Robert pointed out was off by almost a foot.

The officials said something about resetting the hurdles after the women ran and one was off by over eight inches or so. They fixed it."

Griffin has adopted certain tenets he lives by. One is the aforementioned "no pressure, no diamonds." Griffin explains: "It was inspired by the desire to be in pressurized situations, championship games, big moments. If you aren't in those games, you have no chance to win a ring. Thus, no pressure, no diamonds." Another of his tenets is "know your why." Again, Griffin explains: "Know your why was inspired by knowing what you do it for, and that is what helps you overcome. Any obstacle in your way will be conquered because you know why you are doing what you are doing. For me, it's my faith and family… being a light for God's kingdom and providing a better life for my family."

For his part, Lamar head coach Lydell Wilson knew he could not allow Cove's overall team speed to dictate the game. Griffin had set the 110-meter Texas high hurdle record his junior year, clocking a 13.55 run to gold. This was the kind of speed that killed on the football field. In addition, Griffin possessed one of the best arms in high school football that year, which the statistics did not necessarily reflect. Josh Boyce was also a highly talented speedster and Lamar did not want the ball in his hands on punts or kicks. Wilson had already instructed his kickers. "He [Boyce] was good for at least one return for touchdown from punt return or kickoff return so we had no reason to ever let him get an attempt."

On the defensive side for Cove, coordinator Brock had one thing he knew they absolutely could not allow to happen. "It was simple for us. Control Jacquizz Rodgers and not let him singlehandedly beat us. Their quarterback was a junior who we felt hadn't been required to provide a lot of support during the season because Quizz was so good. Our goal was to make the QB beat us. From the film that we had seen we knew Smallwood was strong and athletic, but still, Quizz was just so explosive. Bottom line was that Quizz was the known commodity, and we just couldn't allow him to run free."

The season for Cove had been more challenging than normal due to injuries. DC Brock was constantly plugging holes. "Yes, the Waxahachie game and Aledo were physical for sure, and McKinney Boyd was a war as well. Really from week six on we only had two weeks that I'd characterize as less physical. We had Brownwood week six, Midway week eight, Waco week ten, then Waxahachie to start the playoffs, Boyd week thirteen, Aledo week fourteen, and Lamar Consolidated week fifteen. That's a lot of weeks of heavy collisions right there. And in 2007, although defensively we had five to six guys with decent varsity experience from our 2006 team, we didn't have much depth.

"We were especially thin at outside linebacker where we had played with pretty much one player. He was injured against Waco week ten. For the play-offs, we used a couple of guys from the secondary, and then we moved up a true freshman who had never played defense. We were able to make it with the patchwork and then, by the championship game, the freshman, Brandon Durant, had established himself as the starter." District 16-4A boasted three teams in the top ten going into the season according to *Dave Campbell's Texas Football* magazine. And two of those teams, Copperas Cove and Waco, were coming off appearances in the state championship game the prior year. It was undoubtedly the toughest district in all of 4A.

The bi-district meeting with Waxahachie in 2006 had been a nail biter. It was a repeat in 2007 with Cove prevailing 37-35. After breezing past Dallas Samuel, they ran into a tough McKinney Boyd squad. That's when the Cove defense began to assert itself. One player Brock knew he could count on was his own son, Tanner, the defensive captain. Tanner earned first team All-State honors in Class 4A in 2006 and 2007. After Cove moved up in class to 5A for 2008 Tanner once again earned first team All-State honors-at the linebacker position. He tackled sideline to sideline, and he wanted this championship.

The previous week's contest against Aledo was much the same as Lamar's against LBJ with very little offensive output and tough defense. After being behind 7-0 early at Baylor's Floyd Casey Stadium, the Bulldawgs had relied on the legs of Griffin, Vital, and sophomore running back Brandin Byrd to stage a comeback. The 15-9 score did not reflect the number of opportunities the Aledo offense had to take command of the game. The Bearcats actually went into halftime leading 9-7. Griffin and Byrd managed to move the ball in the second half to take the lead. Then Brock's defense, led by son Tanner and head coach Jack Welch's own son, Steven, showed its veteran experience and stopped several scoring opportunities by Aledo. The Aledo Bearcats were a budding dynasty and went on to win state championships in 2009, 2010, 2011, 2013, 2014, 2016, 2018, 2019 and 2021. They lost 21-20 to College Station High School in the 2017 state title game.

This 2007 title game drew large crowds on both sides. Even Austin LBJ head coach Claude Mathis made the drive up to see how the team that had knocked his bunch out would fare against Cove, and to see Jacquizz Rodgers play his last high school football game. Mathis will never forget that night in Round Rock. "It was so cold, but I couldn't miss seeing Quizz and Griffin. Of all the kids I coached against, the two I have the most respect for are Kyler Murray and Jacquizz Rodgers."

In the stands the fans were hunkering down for a long, cold night. Even the adrenaline rush that comes from pre-kickoff anticipation could not dull the cold. Blankets and quilts were spread down the aisles on top of family and friends who were already adorned in multiple layers of clothing and goose down jackets. As the sun began to set, the stadium lights illuminated the playing field much like a microscope lights up the viewing stage, and such that no detail could be missed, and no mistake could hide. This was State.

Inside the Cove locker room, the players were doing their typical pre-game rituals. Receiver Donral Rousell sat in his locker adjusting his equipment one last time. He tapped his cleats and rocked a little to calm his nerves. This was another shot for a title. "I was nervous and excited all at once. We were ready and I just needed to get on the field. Looking around I could see that we were pumped and ready to take this one. It's what you hope to play for every season but so few actually get to do it."

The Cove defense went over their game plan one more time. They had no intentions of letting Jacquizz Rodgers run wild. It was simple for DC Brock: load the box. Loading the box refers to having as many as eight or more of your eleven defenders near the line of scrimmage in order to stop the run. It adds pressure to the defensive secondary but can be a run stopper and get pressure on the quarterback quickly.

Coach Welch was looking for a psychological edge early. Lamar quarterback DJ Smallwood remembers the Mustangs' first offensive possession. "We lined up and I'm about to start calling signals and all I hear is them yelling 'get Quizz.' At first I was like... what the heck? Then I realized they were loading the box and very serious about shutting down our running attack. It definitely caught me by surprise at first though. I don't recall a defense yelling a guy's name in a game before, ever." The Dawgs defensive scheme seemed to work effectively early on.

Welch remembers it well. "It was always about stopping Rodgers. Get as many hats on him as you can on every play." Much like Caniford and New Braunfels, Welch knew he would be giving something up in return for loading the box. "You just have to accept that you're letting somebody somewhere go in order to focus on Rodgers. There's no way around that. You take that risk."

As the Mustangs headed down the tunnel for warmups, Wilson hurried to the front to halt his troops. He quickly wheeled around to face the players who had stopped suddenly. No words were spoken. He made eye contact with his captains: Smallwood, Obi, Osagiede and Rodgers. His message, though unspoken, was loud and clear. They had prepared for a long time for this moment. The game plan was solid. They would always dance with the one that brought them. There would be no fancy plays, no razzle dazzle. They would win because it's not the biggest dog in the fight that matters, but the biggest fight in the dog. And they would always have the most fight. The lessons from previous failures had been learned. All the necessary sacrifices had been made. After pausing, Wilson released his players to the field for warmups.

As the head coach walked to midfield his steps and his stride were calculated. Every word he spoke and every move he made were statements to his players. They watched him closely. Where did all of that confidence, that swagger, come from? Was this some sort of a Richmond thing? Maybe it came right out of the Heights, where most of these kids were born. Wilson carried a chip on his shoulder of his own. He was young and he was black, and that combination had won very few state championships in Texas. Ronnie Humphrey didn't have to wonder. He came from North Richmond too. He had walked the halls of Pink Elementary like Wilson. He created his dreams at the same little old City Park as Smallwood, Osagiede, and Rodgers had. They all were hatched from the same mold, and they all carried that same DNA down Collins Street and over those same railroad tracks.

The night was Wilson's opportunity to exorcise some demons on behalf of a lot of people. The twin towns of Richmond-Rosenburg had turned out in force to support their native son and his team. Young coaches all over the state were watching and hoping. And a team of young men with Mustangs on their helmets who had bought into his system were looking to finish what they had started. Wilson never flinched. Not once. He couldn't afford to. Copperas Cove was confident too, and loaded with more than enough talent to take this championship.

As the sun started to set, the temperature quickly dove into the teens and the wind was swirling. Sitting on the east side meant staring right into the chilling wind. Warm-ups were over and the two teams had received their last-minute pep talk. As they spilled out onto the field, my eyes were trained on Robert Griffin. I wondered what the Lamar coaches had in mind for him. Likewise, the Mustangs came out behind their emotional leader Sule Osagiede. The Mustang captains were once again Quizz, Sule, DJ, and Chuck. Representing the Dawgs were seniors Troy Vital, Steven Welch, Sean Robertson, and Robert Griffin. The Bulldawgs were in their royal blue and yellow home uniforms. The Mustangs were in their Nike road whites with the blue numbers outlined in silver.

Lamar won the coin toss and elected to receive the opening kickoff. Forty-eight minutes stood between one of these two teams and a state title in Texas Division 1 Class 4-A. As the two teams lined up for the kick, the fans were up from their seats. One could hear the cowbells from the Copperas Cove side. The roar inside the stadium increased as the Cove Bulldawgs huddled up at their thirty and began to pump up the crowd before dispersing into kick formation. Cove's kicker Michael Roell set the ball on the tee and signaled to the referee he was ready to get this show started.

Welch had no qualms about kicking to Rodgers, who fielded the ball at his own goal line and then managed to get back only to the sixteen. The Mustangs came out in a single back set with Rodgers behind Smallwood. On defense Tanner Brock and Jon Smart were the inside linebackers. Tanner called the defensive sets and adjustments. Down on the line was Coach Welch's own son, Steven, at defensive tackle. Reb Brock knew his defense was solid with two coaches' sons in the mix. "Steven was one of the best defensive linemen I've been blessed to coach. He was a player with a high football IQ who understood not only his position but how it fit within our defensive scheme. He was an excellent technician, especially with his hands and body control and was very quick and extremely strong. When you add those pieces together with a guy who played with a chip on his shoulder, it makes for a salty player. Stevo was very salty!"

The Dawg defense had eight men in the box for this opening possession. Their intentions were clear. On first down, Rodgers took the pitch and ran into a host of Cove defenders led by Brock and Smart for a gain of five yards. Continuing in the one back set, Wilson was trying to somehow spread out the Cove defense. On second down, Smallwood faked the handoff to Quizz and darted through the right side of the line behind his big right guard, Presley Godson and right tackle Paul Alford. Quickly into the second level, Smallwood was up to the 34-yard line for the Mustang's initial first down. The

Mustangs continued to grind with another first down at their own 46-yard line. Smallwood attempted a screen pass to Quizz that was almost intercepted by Cove defensive lineman Anthony Gonzalez.

Smallwood followed up with another run to the right side for a first and ten at Cove's 43-yard line. It was becoming clear that keying on Quizz was opening things up for the Mustang quarterback to make the defense pay. After stuffing Quizz on first and second downs, the Mustangs were looking at third and ten. Smallwood faked the handoff and avoided a swarm of Dawgs to get outside the pocket. He spied Travis Riedel at the Cove thirty and fired a bullet. Riedel made a circus catch and toe-touched just in bounds for a huge reception to keep the drive alive. The Mustang sideline came alive. Now it was up to the Dawg defense to slow down the Lamar freight train.

On first down, Quizz took a delayed handoff and was quickly up to the Cove eighteen. The Mustang offense had gotten out of the gate quickly and was looking sharp. The play mix was giving the Dawg defense some issues. The Mustangs got as far as the 11-yard line before running out of luck. The Cove defense became relentless in swarming to Rodgers or pressuring Smallwood into hurried throws. On fourth down, Wilson sent in Adan Gomez for a field goal attempt of twenty-eight yards. The snap was low, and holder Carlos Becerra had to scoop the ball off of the carpet to get it in position. The kick never had a chance and was blocked. Cove recovered at its own eleven and out trotted Robert Griffin III and company.

The Dawgs set up in the power I with Griffin under center and Troy Vital as the tailback. The Mustang offense had chewed up a lot of clock but had nothing to show for it other than knowing they could move the ball. Griffin rolled right and faked to Vital. He then followed his big running back through a hole on the right side for ten-yard gain and Cove's initial first down. The swarming Mustang defense knew to keep Griffin in front of them no matter what. It would be almost impossible to catch the QB with world class speed from behind.

Cove continued in the power I with Griffin receiving the offensive plays from offensive coordinator Tracy Welch on the sideline. The offensive coordinator was head coach Jack Welch's brother. With receivers Tommy Mcleain and Josh Boyce split out to each side, Griffin stepped under center and barked his signals. OC Welch continued to pound his fullback and running back up the middle at the heart of the Mustang defensive line. Defensive tackles Colin Usen and Clarence Ward held their own. On third and ten Griffin took the snap and followed his backs to the left side. Defensive end Andrew Nwaogwugwu appeared to have Griffin at the Dawg twenty, but the elusive quarterback slipped this tackle and got the corner before being run out at the Cove 37-yard line for a huge first down in the opening stanza.

On second down, Troy Vital got going with a quick hitter up the middle to the Mustang 47-yard line. It was a glimpse of what the first team all-state running back was capable of doing when he got into space. Vital, whose running style reminded many pundits of Eric Dickerson, was a no frills, north-south type runner. However, he continued to be hampered with a severe high ankle sprain and had to be spelled by Byrd at times throughout the game. Cove's coaching staff had gotten comfortable with the sophomore in the game. Said Brock: "Brandin was used enough in the season to be reliable. Plus, he showed against Aledo that he was quite capable of making plays in big games."

On first and ten, Byrd came into the game. With Griffin still under center Welch went to a one back set for the first time. There seemed to be some confusion with the offense and Cove was called for illegal procedure, moving the ball back to their own 48-yard line. From the shotgun Griffin gave to Byrd who burst through the middle down to the Lamar forty. Then Griffin was pushed out on a keeper at the 37-yard line by linebacker Justin Goodson who refused to let RG III get to the corner. It was good enough, though, for a new set of downs for the Dawgs offense. On the next play, Byrd appeared to be stopped at the line of scrimmage, but the big sophomore kept his feet moving and took the ball to the Lamar 25-yard line for another big first down. The Cove offense was starting to find some running room for its big three. The quarter came to an end with the Bulldawgs threatening.

After changing ends of the field, it was Troy Vital's turn to bust one, taking it all the way to the Lamar eight. Then the Mustang defense got aggressive and pushed the Cove offense back to the fourteen where, on fourth down, Welch sent in Michael Roell to attempt a thirty-yard field goal. Rodgers set up on the left side for the defense near the center of the field. At the snap Quizz jetted through the line and got a hand on the kick, sending the ball careening through the left side of the end zone for a touchback. The game remained scoreless and Quizz's football prowess was on full display. OC Tracy Welch and the Cove staff were not expecting to see so much of Rodgers. "We were certainly not expecting to see Quizz on defense. He was putting some hard hits on our quarterback."

The Mustang offense continued to flounder and on fourth and twenty Wilson sent in Taylor Turner to punt. The senior punter hit one high and deep from his own ten to the forty of Cove where returner Boyce misjudged it and let it go over his head. Boyce ran back and scooped the ball up at his own twenty where he escaped the tackle of Andrew Okokhere. He then headed up field and split the coverage team at midfield. Eluding several would-be tacklers, he made it all the way back to the Lamar forty where Carlos Becerra and Quentin Palmer stopped him. It was a nervous moment for the Lamar sideline.

On first down, Griffin was quickly down to the 30-yard line with plenty of time in the second quarter. Just as quickly, Cove fumbled on the next play and Quizz recovered it and was taken down at the Lamar thirty. Mistakes were becoming costly for both teams in the first half. Not discouraged, Welch and Brock continued to attack the football on every down. Smallwood could not get enough time to find his receivers and Lamar punted again. Cove continued to win field position and had another opportunity before the half from their own forty.

Griffin connected on first down to Boyce to move the markers to Lamar's own 45-yard line. He then tried to get the ball to Rousell, but Rodgers darted in and timed it perfectly. His hit from the strong safety position jarred the ball loose and knocked the wind out of the Cove receiver. Rousell recalls being in the game against Quizz. "What defined him was his strength. He was an ox. He was their ace in the hole. He was playing offense and defense, and he was very active on both sides of the ball. He made his presence felt on defense for sure. And then, there he was breaking the touchdown record on offense. It was crazy."

Just when the Mustang defense thought they had Griffin contained, he scrambled out of trouble on third and long and found Boyce on the Lamar sideline for a strike and big first down. With first and goal at the Lamar seven, Cove lined up in the power I with under two minutes to play in the first half. On first down, Vital was met at the line of scrimmage by Clarence Ward for no gain. The Lamar defense had been stellar for two quarters and wanted to go into half time having kept Cove out of the end zone. On second down, Griffin tried a keeper up the middle but hit a wall. He bounced it to the outside to his right but just as he attempted to cross the five, he was met by Palmer who rode the Dawg quarterback out of bounds at the four. With time running out OC Tracy Welch had the perfect offensive call in mind. When the play was signaled in, Boyce knew it was his time to make something happen. "Coach Welch used us the right way. We had a special play just for that game and for that specific situation."

Welch sent out both Vital and Byrd into the backfield with Griffin in the shotgun. Boyce was split out to the right. Griffin called a shift and went under center. Vital and Byrd moved out of the backfield and into position to the left of the offensive line in the slot. It was an unusual set and one Lamar had not seen. Griffin crouched down under center and started his cadence. Boyce went into motion from the right side of the field and, just as he was about to cross behind Griffin to his left, the ball was snapped, and Griffin flipped it to Boyce who quickly tucked it in. Vital and Byrd got their blocks and Boyce had a slim lane into the end zone which he quickly filled. Just like that, Copperas Cove was on the board. Mike Roell's point after was good and, with just 36.1 seconds remaining in the first half, the Copperas Cove Bulldawgs were finally on the board.

COP. COVE	7
LAMAR CON	0

The temperature continued to drop throughout the first half until the wind chill was near zero. The two teams had barely noticed because the competition was so fierce. My toes were frozen in spite of a double layer of socks. The huddled mass of fans on the Lamar side, covered up with blankets, were suddenly quiet. The folks on the opposite side were up on their feet and screaming. The cowbells they vigorously shook were even more annoying now. The Bulldawg cheerleaders turned cartwheels and waved their blue pompoms wildly as their team had finally put the ball in the end zone. After several weeks of scrambling to get past opponents, the Cove faithful were accustomed to these sorts of battles.

Lamar, however, was not used to being held scoreless. Even in close contests, the Mustangs had been able to put some points on the board. Cove DC Reb Brock had dialed up the perfect answer to Lydell Wilson's potent running attack. Even when the Mustangs had gone to quarterback DJ Smallwood, they had not done any better than an attempted field goal, which was blocked. Cove had stuffed Rodgers and forced turnovers to keep the potent

Mustang scoring attack silent. Jacquizz Rodgers had come into the contest looking to lead his team to the promise land and extend his state record in touchdowns. Neither had happened up to that point.

Lamar cornerback Quentin Palmer remembers going into halftime not overly concerned about the late Cove score. "At that point in the season we were so battle tested that there was never a sense of anxiety or added pressure that maybe we were in a situation we couldn't handle. I remember as a defense we were very relaxed in the state game specifically."

In the Mustang locker room, the coaching staff quickly split the players into position groups to discuss their second half intentions. There was no panic, just calm resolve to get things going on both sides of the ball. They had to take the heat off of Quizz. Wilson asked quarterback Smallwood to step up and use his legs. Offensive Coordinator Matthews drew it up for the offense. "As a coaching staff we decided to use Quizz as a decoy and feature Smallwood and do play action pass off of that. If that worked then we could go back to Quizz when they keyed on Smallwood."

For the defense, there really was not any sense from the coaches that anything needed to be done differently. The defensive game plan was still solid, and Wilson never really worried about that side of the ball. "We just told the defense to keep hitting Griffin and not letting him in space. They had done a good job for the most part. The touchdown just before the half really didn't change anything because we had done such a good job to that point. Our defense had done its job."

From Cove's perspective the game was going the way they had intended. Welch had Griffin moving the offense and Brock's defense was pitching a shutout. Said Welch: "It was still the same plan— limit what Rodgers did when they had the ball, and get first downs on offense. There really wasn't much to think about. We were doing what we wanted. Really, we just needed to keep doing exactly what we had done in the first half."

As Rodgers trotted to the tunnel leading into the warm locker room, he could not help but think how familiar it all was. Here he was, once again, so close but still so far. He was doing everything humanly possible. On both sides of the ball. But the football gods were demanding more. They seemed to enjoy seeing the limits of the human spirit. Rodgers was determined as ever to not disappoint. He never did.

CHAPTER 13

A TALE OF TWO HALVES

Halftime from the stands was all about coping with the bone-chilling wind that was swirling in from the north. As far as football goes, from the Lamar perspective, the questions on everybody's mind were: How in the world would they get Quizz going? How much longer could they keep Griffin under wraps? Cove's late score was still stinging when I heard somebody playing music loud enough that I could hear it from where I sat several seats away. I recognized the lyrics and realized how apropos Kid Rock was at that moment. Sometimes only God knows why.

As the halftime clock closed in on double zeros, the teams prepared to take the field. The Lamar coaches had made only a few changes. For the most part they just reminded the Mustangs of their game plan and going back out and doing their thing. Coach Wilson had one simple concept in mind for this particular halftime. "We really didn't have anything major to change on either side of the ball. We pretty much stayed with our game plan all the way through. All I said to the players was don't let the game be bigger than what it was, which was my usual." Coach Matthews added, "We made some minor blocking changes and moved some people around."

Linebacker Justin Goodson saw a locker room filled with confidence in spite of the score. "We were pretty calm. Never even considered we could lose. Coach Wilson got us pumped up and we were itching to get back out there and perform."

D'Vonn Brown was one of only a few sophomores who played regularly during the playoff run. He remembered seeing all of his team and coaching staff acting calm. "I never saw anything other than complete confidence.

Really, there is only so much the coaches can change at halftime. Plus, there really wasn't anything that had changed during the course of the first half. On defense, we needed to continue to control Griffin. I knew they had to get Quizz going on offense. But they had DJ too and he had always come through during the season when things weren't going good otherwise. We knew the coaches were going to figure things out."

Quarterback Smallwood became the focus of the coaching staff. Wilson was emphatic that his junior signal caller get more aggressive in the second half. Smallwood recalls: "The coaches and really the whole locker room was calm, but this was not what we had come to do. No way we go out like this. Coach Wilson was telling me to step up and lead this team. He challenged me to do more."

Coach Hummel had come down from the sky box and was not mincing words.

Hummel: Deeeeeee jayyyyyyy

Smallwood: Yes, Coach?

Hummel: What the hell are you doing? They are totally keying on Quizz! The run is there, use your legs. Stop pussyfooting around. You're blowing this!

Smallwood: Yes sir, Coach Hum

The quarterback bent over and retied the laces of his Nikes. Then he stood up and adjusted his shoulders pads underneath his number 15 jersey, and said to himself, "Okay, I know what time it is." He walked outside the locker room and the frigid air filled his helmet. He had forgotten about that. Suddenly, the lighted scoreboard caught his gaze.

ROUND ROCK ISD		
COP. COVE.	12:00	LAMAR CON
7		0

And just as quickly, the cold evaporated from his mind. Twenty-four minutes left in this one. This night would not get away from him. Not like last season in this very same stadium. He squinted at the scoreboard and his mind became razor sharp. It was actually quite simple. Call the plays, give Quizz the ball or make good reads and sharp passes. And if the opening were there, he would run. There would be no hesitation. Suddenly, his legs felt strong. The adrenaline flowed through his veins. He was the quarterback, the commander-in-chief to his troops. He would lead them. The plan was still intact. Darrell Smallwood Jr. did, indeed, know what time it was. It was his job to go out and dismantle Copperas Cove.

Defensive end Deante Ester felt the team was hanging tough. "We just said… hey we are in a dogfight with a really good team. Just keep playing hard. We knew we just needed to keep doing what we were already doing. There really were no adjustments. We tended to wear people down. We just needed to outlast them."

Linebacker Cory Green kept his focus on the same plan they had going into the contest. "Do not let Robert Griffin beat us. We knew how great a runner he was. We were determined to keep him behind the line of scrimmage, running him sideline to sideline. Hit him on every play."

As per usual, Osagiede led the team down the tunnel and back onto the playing surface. And as was also the norm, he turned one last time to yell his mantra. "One for all, all for one. Won't be beat, can't be beat. One more meal, gentlemen, and we're full."

In the opposite locker room, there was also a calm anticipation. With the scoring play before half, the Dawgs had finally gotten Griffin and the offense going. For their part, Coach Brock's defense had kept the most prolific running back in the state of Texas out of the end zone. The game plan going forward was more of the same according to Head Coach Welch. "I told them we are halfway there. Just go out and continue to play solid defense, continue to get first downs on offense. Get some more points on the board and control the clock as we had. I told them there were twenty-four more minutes of football to be played and I knew they would give it their all. I was proud of them, and I loved each and every one."

But inside his mind, Welch had no delusions that he could stand pat. He knew full well that the opposing coaching staff had most likely made some adjustments. "Oh, I knew they were very good at making halftime adjustments so we would wait for them to show their hand before making our own adjustments. They had already shown against LBJ that they were willing to split Rodgers out to open things up. As we prepared to take the field for the third quarter, I just told them to keep their heads in the game and play their hearts out."

Tracy Welch was confident going into the second half. Griffin had fought through, and overcome, in the prior game an Aledo defense that was hell bent on stopping him. Even when Cove abandoned any semblance of disguising the fact that they were going to put the game in Robert Griffin's hands, the Bearcat defense still was unable to stop him. Just as he had when harnessed to a tire while running uphill all of the way, he could put the Cove offense on his back when needed. There was no reason for anything to be any different in the second half of the title game. Twenty-four minutes.

As the Dawgs stood one last time to exit the locker room as a team, Griffin could not help but feel somewhat nostalgic. The Mustangs had kept him under wraps in the first half, but every team had some success by keying on him. Eventually, a mistake was always made and then he would showcase his world class speed. His team had a lead. Now it was time to put some nails in the coffin. He fidgeted with the glove on his left hand, redoing the strap much like a batter stepping in and out of the batter's box in baseball. He looked around and saw his best friends. It was time to win.

The first half of the state championship had been anything but uneventful. Some great defensive play was taking center stage in a game that featured two high profile offensive players in Rodgers and Griffin. As is usually the case, offense makes the headlines and defense wins championships. Just before the Mustangs left the tunnel one last time, Consolidated coach Lane Wade made one final plea. Jonathon Taylor remembers the defensive coordinator calling the players together. "He asked us if we came all of this way to lose. He said our small town was shut down and everybody had come all this way with us. Did we want to let them down? He said he knew some of us had been playing together since we were young and did we want to let each other down? It was more emotion than we had seen out of coach Wade ever."

The Bulldawgs received the second half kickoff at their own 30-yard line after another pooch kick by Lamar to avoid Josh Boyce. The Dawgs were unable to get anything going out of the half and punted early. The Mustangs set up shop at their own twelve, and with two quarters to go, Wilson needed to figure out exactly how to manufacture some points in this second half. "It wasn't a matter of necessarily doing something totally different in the second half. At that point you just had to get your kids to execute. The same things they had been doing all year."

At one point, Smallwood put Rodgers in motion and, after rolling to his left, threw a quick pass to Quizz out in the left flat. Cove free safety Rashad Hardy swooped in and had an interception. He was taken down at the Lamar 27-yard line. Griffin and company hurried on the field ready to take advantage of the turnover. It was a golden opportunity to get on top of the Mustangs before they had a chance to get any momentum. Four downs later, the Bulldawgs gave it right back. The Lamar defense was not going to let Griffin get going either. After two runs by Quizz, the Mustangs were facing a third and short. Smallwood took a keeper and got through the left side of the line behind a pulling Paul Alford and made it to the Lamar forty-four and a new set of downs. The junior QB would need to keep this up for the Mustangs to have any chance of success on offense.

Smallwood knew in 2006 that he probably had not put his best foot forward in the loss to Alamo Heights. "The Alamo Heights loss was very humbling in so many ways. After being undefeated and with so much talent around me, we were suddenly touchable. It showed me that someone who wants it more than you do can easily take it away." The Mustang quarterback was determined not to let this one slip away. He could not set back and wait for somebody else to make things happen. It was now or never.

On first down, Smallwood got taken down for a loss by defensive tackle Welch back at the Lamar 39-yard line. The next offensive play ultimately changed the course of the contest. Smallwood faked once again to Quizz and appeared to attempt to get the corner near the Lamar sideline. The box was stacked, and the Cove defense had the junior signal caller dead in his tracks. Smallwood quickly pulled up and fired to his 6-foot 180-pound tight end Dominique Briggs at the Lamar 45-yard line for a surprise pass in the flat. Briggs quickly turned up field and ran over the first Cove defender. He juked the second Dawg and scooted along the Mustang sideline before being pushed out at the Cove 43-yard line for a first down. Suddenly, the defensive box was a little less crowded.

First and ten. The Cove defense kept barking, only now it was not *Get Quizz*. Now the chatter was at each other and who had who.

Who's got the tight end? Who's got 85?

On the next snap, Smallwood once again put his offense in a one back set and glanced at Briggs. He took the snap, faked the dive play to Quizz to the right side, and the Cove defense swarmed to their left. At the last second, Smallwood pulled the ball back and shot the left gap quickly into the

Cove secondary where he eluded several defenders before being hauled down at the Cove 31-yard line. Again, the box was getting less crowded, and the chatter got a little louder.

Who's got the QB? Who's got 15?

Cove was finding out what LBJ and New Braunfels had discovered. Wilson would use all of his playmakers when needed. They could not just load the box. The quarterback dumped to his big tight end or used misdirection to get himself in space. All of this came with fakes to Rodgers. Suddenly the Dawgs found themselves on their heels. A defense that had played so well in the first half now had to deal with not one, but three weapons on the Lamar offense. All of this led to one thing, of course. On the next play, Smallwood handed to Quizz, who stutter stepped through the left center-guard gap and barreled into a Cove linebacker who missed. Rodgers then sprinted upfield as though he was headed straight into the Cove safeties waiting for him at their own 22-yard line. The first one missed as Quizz quickly changed directions, but the second defender grabbed him around his legs. Rodgers' legs were churning hard, and he broke this tackle and ran towards the right side of the Cove end zone. He accelerated to score Consolidated's first touchdown of the contest. With Gomez's extra point good, the game was now tied, and the Copperas Cove defense had a problem with 2:45 left in the third quarter.

COP. COVE	7
LAMAR CON	7

On the other side of the ball, the Mustang defense continued to swarm on Griffin, and kept him running laterally, trying to keep him from getting into space. On first down, he took the snap from the shotgun and was immediately met by Ester and Ward who dragged him down for a seven-yard loss. Griffin was exasperated as he picked himself up yet again from the cold, hard Round Rock playing surface. On second down, Griffin went under center with Vital behind him in the I-formation. He took the snap and handed to his running back who was immediately dropped for a loss by Osagiede. Third and seventeen. Griffin was forced to throw it away on third down and Cove had to punt.

Smallwood brought his offense to the line at Lamar's own seven. Welch once again was all over Quizz for no gain on first down, and he appeared to have Smallwood for a sack until the quarterback found his tight end Briggs along the Lamar sideline. Smallwood quickly lofted the ball to Briggs who turned and ran to the 18-yard line. The third quarter came to an end and the Mustangs offense had found some answers.

After changing sides of the field, the Mustangs came right back to Smallwood. From the shotgun he took the snap and headed to his right. He quickly cleared the line of scrimmage and got outside. At the forty, he encountered safety Rashad Hardy. Smallwood dipped his shoulder and planted Hardy on his back. He was finally run out of bounds at the Lamar forty-eight. Wilson stayed with the hot hand, and Smallwood was soon to the Cove side of the field for another big first down. Next, he danced his way around the left side to Cove's thirty-seven. After a five-yard run by Rodgers, Smallwood carried again to the twenty. The junior QB was chewing up yardage in chunks as the Cove defense continued to key on Quizz.

After Smallwood carried to the Cove eight, the Mustangs were looking at a first and goal. Rodgers took the hand off and followed his tight end Briggs through the right side of the line. He was met by several Cove defenders at the five. He spun out of these attempted tackles and ran backwards into the end zone. The play became known as the "moon walk" touchdown and it put Lamar up for the first time in the contest. Gomez made the point after with 7:56 remaining in the final stanza of this championship game.

COP. COVE	7
LAMAR CON	**14**

With over half the quarter left to go, the Cove offense needed to respond. Kicking away from Boyce had given Griffin and his offense good starting position all night. On the next drive, Griffin set things up at the Cove forty-four. Wilson was willing to give up field position to keep Boyce from doing any damage. It was frustrating for the junior receiver. "I felt I could change the game on any given punt return," recalls Boyce.

Coach Welch sent his senior out firing away, and on third down Griffin connected with Boyce on a crossing pattern that took the ball to the Lamar thirty-one. Then he rolled right and fired complete to receiver Rousell at Lamar's twenty. Cove was looking to answer and quickly.

Griffin found receiver Tommy Mcleain next for another big gain and a first and goal at the nine. On first down, Griffin used his legs to buy some time, but the receivers were covered up, so he tucked and kept down to the four. Second down was a designed quarterback draw, but Griffin was met quickly by Osagiede for no gain. On third down, Griffin faked to Byrd and tried to squeeze a pass in between Obi and Rodgers to Boyce in the end zone. Rodgers deflected the pass for an incompletion. Now the Bulldawgs were looking at fourth and goal at their own four.

Rather than attempt a field goal, Welch looked to tie this game up and keep the momentum going from this big drive. Griffin was in the shotgun with Byrd to his right, Mcleain in the slot, and Boyce split out wide right. With the snap, he immediately rolled to his right, ball cocked for the throw. Boyce and Mcleain were covered up in the end zone. Griffin saw that he had the corner behind a big block by Byrd. What he did not see was the fact that Lamar linebacker Cory Green was sitting on the play with just Griffin to worry about. Green remembers it as the best play of his high school career.

"We figured Rob would run it even though he sold the pass. It was just a matter of which side he went to. I immediately realized they were blocking the play towards my side, which was to their right. I just had to make sure I didn't get blocked or caught up in traffic. He never saw me, and I popped him at the three and got him out of bounds at the two." It was a stunning end to a very promising drive. On top of that there now were only a few minutes left in the game. Cove needed to keep this field position and get the ball back in Griffin's hands quickly.

With the Mustang faithful stomping their feet in the stands and screaming as loud as they collectively could, the Lamar offense took the field at their own 2-yard line knowing they had just been handed a gift. The Dawg defense lined up, somewhat stunned by Lamar's goal line stand. The first-down play was a handoff to Quizz, who got out to the nine and out of the shadow of his own goal line. Lamar needed to milk some clock and put some distance between the Cove offense and their own end zone. On second down, Quizz made it to the thirteen for a precious first down.

Time was beginning to be a factor now for the Dawgs and they knew it. They did not have the luxury of merely slowing the Mustang offense down. They needed a stop and to get the ball back into Griffin's hands. The Dawg offense proved they could move the ball and they needed to put the missed opportunity behind them and come roaring back. Still, Wilson felt the Cove defense was vulnerable and the best play would always be to Quizz.

Said Wilson: "You know there were not that many possessions in the first half. We had been sticking to our game plan and ran what we worked on all week. With the wind and the weather there were not going to be a lot of passes thrown for either side." Smallwood huddled his team and called their bread-and-butter play: "Iso right on two." The offense went into formation and DJ started his cadence. "Blue 22… blue 22… hut hut." And then it happened.

I had made my way down to the North end zone to get my blood pumping and try getting the feeling back in my toes. I was chatting with some Lamar faithful when suddenly I saw Quizz had broken through the line at his own 13-yard line. I stood there frozen, not because of the cold, but because I realized Quizz was in the secondary and had gotten behind… everybody. I found myself talking out loud to nobody in particular "He's broken free… they won't catch him." I stood there motionless, totally forgetting to breathe as Rodgers came closer and closer.

Quizz took the handoff from Smallwood and started right but was immediately grabbed by Cove defensive end Antony Cotton. Quizz shrugged off this tackle and broke back toward the middle of the line of scrimmage. Cove linebacker Brock had stayed home and had the play covered, except Coach Matthews' blocking scheme was on point with right guard Presley Godson pulling. Brock and Godson collided at the line of scrimmage. Quizz immediately recognized the situation: a scene he had witnessed thousands of times in his high school career. A defense had over-pursued in their desperate attempt to box him in. The pulling block of Godson had created a sliver of a gap, a microsecond of an opportunity. It was at this moment when anticipation and muscle memory took the reins, and just like that, Quizz made his patented cut-back move.

Then… daylight.

The sudden emergence of Rodgers to the second level caught the Cove secondary by surprise. Still, two Cove defenders were within a few feet of Rodgers as he headed towards the Lamar end zone eighty-seven yards away. This Cove team was loaded with state ranked track talent and this was going to be a race for the championship. By the time Rodgers crossed his own goal line he had put another few yards between himself and the two Dawg defenders chasing him.

He ran faster than he had ever run before. He would not be caught. Not here, not on this night. Not after all those hours spent in the field house doing squats, dead lifts, and power cleans. Not after all those hot, muggy summer days running 100-yard sprints, alone with only his thoughts and dreams to keep him company. Not after all those running plays late in the fourth quarter of games long since put away. The fans sometimes questioned Coach Wilson's reasons for having Rodgers in games late when it seemed meaningless and possibly risking injury. But Wilson knew this moment would come. The moment when he needed his guy to be better than everybody else. No, Jacquizz Rodgers would not be caught. He ran... to glory.

COP. COVE	7
LAMAR CON	20

The stunned crowd on the Cove side fell silent. The Dawg fans had been caught flat-footed as they were still trying to dissect the goal line stand by the Mustang defense. And suddenly they had to witness their worst fear. They had heard the rumors. They knew this was always a possibility. But had it actually just happened right before their eyes? All they could do was turn to each other and ask the proverbial question: What the hell just happened? The extra point was no good and the Mustangs now had a 20-7 lead. With 2:43 left in the contest the Dawgs needed a miracle. And if anybody could pull it off, it was Griffin. He had done that very thing the previous week against a state-ranked defense in Aledo. Surely, he had a chance against this unheralded bunch of Mustangs. But Coach Welch would have to unleash his guy on every play. Tasked with running out the clock, Wilson elected to have Gomez kick deep. Boyce fielded the kick at his own five. At the 30-yard line he encountered a slew of Mustangs. Suddenly he cut to his left and accelerated into open field. Just as he was about to separate from the defenders, Lamar's Julius Smith lunged for a shoestring tackle. Boyce leapt up quickly and punched the air. One more inch and it would have been six points for the Dawgs. On the Lamar sideline Wilson realized he had stopped breathing. It was the first time all night he questioned his own decision making.

The Cove offense quickly took the field. The thinking in football is that when you need multiple scores you only think about getting the first one.

And that was the only thing on Robert Griffin's mind. Cove made no attempt to disguise their intentions. Griffin was in the shotgun. They would ride his arm and legs one final time. But after heavy pressure from an energized Mustang defense, Griffin threw three consecutive incompletions. Cove was now facing fourth down. Flushed once again to his left, Griffin found Rousell in the flat near the Lamar sideline, but well short of a first down. The Lamar players were shouting at their defense to get Rousell down. But the fleet-footed Rousell juked several defenders and made his way to the Cove 47-yard for a first down.

On first down, Griffin's pass attempt was knocked down by Osagiede. However, Lamar was called for a personal foul, moving the ball to the Mustang forty and an automatic first. Then Griffin launched a bomb down to Boyce at the five. All the Mustangs could do was tackle Boyce, who had gotten wide open. The resulting penalty gave Cove a first at the Lamar 25-yard line and, more importantly, had preserved precious seconds on the game clock for the Dawgs. On the next play, Griffin went back to Boyce at the Lamar 15. Boyce shook off several tacklers and made it to the Mustang 3-yard line.

On first and goal, Welch went back to the fly sweep that had gotten the Dawgs their touchdown just before the half. Seeing the defense was not fooled, Griffin faked the pitch and attempted a throw into the end zone. But once again, linebacker Green was zeroed in on Griffin and knocked the pass down. At this point, Welch inserted his hard running sophomore and Byrd carried it in for the touchdown to put Cove within one score to win or tie. With only 59.6 seconds left in regulation, the only option Copperas Cove had was to attempt an onside kick. Wilson sent out his "hands" team to receive.

Suddenly visions of the Mayde Creek game entered my mind. Had Cove seen that film? Would they try something similar? How could Lamar let Cove score so quickly after such a stellar game up to that point? As Roell situated the ball on the kicking tee, five Dawgs lined up near the Lamar sideline and five near the Cove side. The Mustangs would have no idea which way the kick was headed. Both sides of the stadium rocked as everybody rose to their feet to cheer their side on. This was probably going to decide the contest. I said a short prayer under my breath as Roell raised his right hand to signal to the referee that his team was ready.

The Cove kicker approached the ball and sent it skipping towards the Mustang side of the field. The Cove defenders near the Lamar sideline obviously knew the kick was coming their way as they sent several guys forward to get in front of the bouncing ball just as it neared the required ten yards. This was meant to create confusion with the Mustangs and allow the Dawgs trailing to try and catch a lucky bounce. However, the ball hung up for just a second and seemed to slow down in the air. Lamar's Chuck Obi recognized what had happened and immediately sprinted out to snatch the ball out of mid-air. The move totally caught the Dawg defenders by surprise and Obi got to Cove's 40-yard line before he wisely slid down.

With less than a minute left in the game, it was now up to the Mustangs to run out the clock and put this championship in the books. Coach Welch had managed to hang on to a couple of timeouts, so Lamar would need to run a few plays. Wilson sent his offense out in the power I with Osagiede in at fullback. On first down, Smallwood handed to Rodgers who managed five yards off right tackle. Reb Brock had everybody on defense up at the line. There was no need to guess where things were going from this point forward. And then on second down Smallwood and Rohde mishandled the snap and the ball hit the ground.

The center-quarterback snap is one of the most fundamental of operations in football. Every single play requires the center to get the ball into somebody else's hands. Usually, the quarterback is either under center or in the shotgun. In situations like this, most coaches will have the QB under center to decrease the chances of a fumble. Yet, there the football sat, between Rohde's feet as he held his ground from the charge of the Cove defensive lineman. Somehow Smallwood had managed to dive straight down and recover the fumbled ball. Welch called another quick timeout.

On third down. Smallwood got a clean snap and tossed to Rodgers who weaved his way to the Cove 31-yard line. Another quick time out. Now it was fourth and one. After the timeout Smallwood quickly brought his offense to the line. Cove had ten men on the line. They seemed to guess that the play would be to their left, and they guessed correctly. As Quizz received the pitch, he was immediately swallowed up by several blitzing Cove defenders. But suddenly he broke away and charged across the line carrying several defenders with him. They finally managed to take him down at the Cove 28-yard line. First down. No more time outs.

As the final seconds clicked off the Round Rock scoreboard, I found myself methodically searching out specific players one by one. First Quizz, then Sule, Obi, Palmer, Ester, and on and on. And then Wilson. I wanted to take it all in with each individual. This miracle had finally happened. I had to keep watching so that it had to be real. Slowly the Copperas Cove play-ers formed a single file line at midfield and one by one the two teams con-gratulated each other. And then the on-field celebration began. There was no holding back. The team towels waived high in the air and the tears flowed.

Quizz's third touchdown of the night extended his then state record to 136 career touchdowns. It capped a 241-yard night on thirty-one carries. Quizz had saved his best for last. His third touchdown, an 87-yard all-out sprint in which he busted through tackles and then separated from a very fast Cove secondary, was emblematic of his entire career. They gave Quizz the ball and he scored touchdowns. He used his low center of gravity to make himself impossible to arm tackle. He used his vision to make preci-sion open field cuts and leave would-be tacklers grabbing air. And he used his acceleration and sprinter's speed to run away from most defenses. It was always a thing of beauty. But for Rodgers, it could have been just another touchdown, no different from the previous 135. He never boasted. He might give his O-line some love or thank his coaches for believing in him. His demeanor never changed.

The last touchdown of Rodgers' high school career cemented his legacy as a Texas high school football legend. His coach took to calling him Mr. Touch-down. And he was named the 2007 Built Ford Tough Class 4A Player of the Year. *Texas Football* made him their inaugural Texas State Player of the Year.

Josh Boyce knew he had been watching the best player in the state. But still, Cove had their chances. "We had the game right where we wanted it. We let a very good football team hang around instead of putting them away when we had the chance. It goes without saying that there were some lost opportunities on our side."

In the end, Plan B was the perfect plan. But who were these boys of 2007? What made them different from all of the great teams they defeated? How were they able to accomplish what a more talented 2006 Mustang team couldn't? They were symbolic of the kid who got picked fifth or sixth during a schoolyard football game. The guy who was not supposed to have enough talent to beat out the "obviously" more talented kids. They were the kid who didn't care who some guy's father was or what car or truck some-body drove to school. All they cared about was earning that spot on the team and winning.

At some point in the season, they had all become too emotionally invested in the championship to be turned back. They had emerged from the locker room after the half exuding a cool confidence. One would have thought they were sitting on a comfortable lead instead of being down a score. Their swagger had actually made me nervous. When Osagiede strutted up and down the sideline getting loose, all the while glaring at the Cove bench, I had wanted to yell at him to go sit down and stop stirring the pot. But that's not who those Mustangs were.

They had to work harder. They had to care more. They had to make the coach's decision to start them an easy one. They left no doubt. Once they got into the starting lineup nothing was going to take that away. They had a chip on their shoulder that probably transcended the football field into their private lives. To outsiders and pundits their names were hard to remember because they were not "blue-chips" or "D-1".

Suddenly it was not so difficult to remember Ester, Palmer, Becerra, Smallwood, Pena, Briggs, and Quintanilla. Even names like "Wah-goo-goo" and "O-saw-ga-day" started to roll off the tongue. Names like Fleming and Godson dotted the all-state roster, but still they were just those hometown guys. They had fought through everything to get to a championship, and it was theirs forever. In Coach Wilson's own words: "They're champions now, and nobody can ever take that away from them."

For his part, Quizz had proven the pundits wrong once again. His 5'7" frame did not seem so "diminutive." If anything, 2007 and, more specifically, this night showed he was larger than life. His stat sheet for the night read like this:

> 31 carries for 241 yards rushing
>
> 3 touchdowns
>
> 6 tackles
>
> 1 fumble caused
>
> 1 fumble recovered
>
> 1 blocked field goal
>
> Several passes broken up

Rodgers missed only two plays the entire game when his chin strap broke. Wilson almost called a time-out. He wanted his star on the field. "Quizz changed the whole mentality of the defense that night. He loved contact, and when on defense he had a little bit of a mean streak."

Williams: DJ, Brandon Williams from the Houston Chronicle. It was rough sledding out there in the first half, but it seemed the coaches got you more involved and that opened up things for your running back.

Smallwood: Yessir. The coaches came up to me at halftime and said I needed to step up and lead this team, use my legs to soften up their defense. I wanted to prove to everyone that I was able to lead a team to a state championship. They keyed on Jacquizz all night long, and I wanted to show them that he wasn't the only threat in the backfield.

Williams: Jacquizz, they had your number in the first half, but you got it going in the second half.

Rodgers: Nah, man, this was the plan. We did this for ourselves, for our coaches, and for all those people up there in the stands who never gave up on us. This is just how I planned it. This was the plan all along.

Williams: Coach, y'all just won the school's first state championship in football. How does it feel?

Wilson: Feels great. I always dreamed of bringing a championship to my hometown.

Williams: They had your number in the first half but then you got your running back going.

Wilson: That right there... #33... hands down ... bar none ... best football player in the state of Texas. When I get on the bus I'm going to cry, because he's going to be gone.

AFTERWORD

The 2007 championship is Lamar Consolidated's lone title in football to date. After Quizz, Sule and the class of 2008 graduated, the Mustangs returned to their normal pattern of being very competitive in district play but not in the playoffs. Quizz went on to join his brother, James, at Oregon State, where they both became stars. He was drafted after his junior year by the Atlanta Falcons. His eight-year pro career included stints with the Chicago Bears and the Tampa Bay Buccaneers. After football, Quizz went back to school and received his diploma from Oregon State. He now lives in Houston with his wife, Samantha, and their children.

Sule Osagiede went to Tulane University on a football scholarship. He had ACL surgery in the spring of 2008. I remember sitting in the stands of Traylor for the 2008 spring football game and Sule came out of the field house on crutches with his newly repaired ACL, smiling the whole time of course. On the morning of Thursday, January 21, 2010, as he was driving home, Osagiede died from injuries he sustained in a car accident in Beaumont, Texas. The news of their fallen warrior was crushing for his Mustang teammates. The one affectionately referred to as "Suk" had been taken way too soon. Nobody from that 2007 championship team had touched people the way Osagiede had. The loss devastated a community and his band of brothers.

Tragedy also struck free safety Steven Fleming who died on January 8, 2010 from injuries he sustained from an accidental gunshot wound. Steven was one of the more easygoing players I got to know. One would never know the level of his talent if you did not meet him on the football field. Like Sule, Steven seemed to have a perpetual smile.

LCISD built a fourth high school, George Ranch, in 2010. It effectively stripped a lot of talent from Lamar Consolidated High School. One only has to look at the fact that GR won a state championship in football in 2015 in only their second year of varsity competition as proof. The new high school hastened the exit of Mustang head coach Lydell Wilson who took over the reins of C.E. King in Houston. Wilson laments what could have been. "We would have gotten the talent that went over to George Ranch. We could have won several more championships."

Nothing, however, can ever take away the championship won by the Mighty Mustangs of 2007. As improbable as it seemed at the time, in hindsight one can see how these young men and their coaches pulled it off. They refused to lose. There were at least five teams that year in Division I Class 4A who could have just as easily won the championship. But they didn't. I often wonder if the young men who gather at City Park in Richmond, Texas for pee wee football talk about the 2007 Mustangs. Do they fight for the number 33 jersey? Do they argue about who gets to be DJ \? Do they talk about the fierceness of Prince Sule?

TERMINOLOGY

Box: the imaginary rectangular space that would theoretically encompass both the offensive and defensive linemen; the line of scrimmage.

Empty set: an offensive formation where only the quarterback is in the backfield behind the center. Everybody else is on the line of scrimmage or split out beyond the offensive line.

In space: used to describe a player with the football who is free to run, make moves, etc. once they have moved beyond the line of scrimmage; in the field of play with the ball with no defenders close by.

In the slot: lined up between the player at the end of the offensive line and the wideout who is near the sideline.

Overloading/Stacking the box: a defensive tactic of placing more than the normal seven defenders close to the line of scrimmage in order to stop running plays.

Pick: an interception by the defender.

Pick six: an interception that is then returned for a touchdown by the defender thereby scoring six points for the defense.

Pooch kick/punt: a tactic whereby the punter/kicker kicks the ball high, short and often towards the sideline to keep it out of the hands of the returner.

Used often to keep the ball out of the hands of a player who is known to be an excellent return man.

Power I: an offensive formation where the quarterback is under center with the fullback behind him and the running back behind his fullback.

Second level: describes an area of the field that is beyond the line of scrimmage, such as in the secondary.

Shotgun: offensive formation where the quarterback is standing upright several yards behind the center and receives the ball via the long snap.

Touches: having the ball in one's hands such as after a handoff, after a caught pass, or after receiving a punt or kickoff.

Under center: offensive formation where the quarterback is squatting directly behind the center with his hands touching the center so as to receive the snap directly.

Wildcat: an offensive formation where someone other than the quarterback lines up in the shotgun and receives the snap directly from the center via a long snap.

ACKNOWLEDGMENTS

This book was a collaboration of gigantic proportions. From the people who were directly involved, to the many who gave advice somewhere along the way. Resurrecting a story thirteen years after the fact was no easy task. And I had no idea a pandemic was right around the corner. Somehow, through numerous instant messages, e-mails and phone calls we managed to pull it off.

Obviously, it all hinged on the players and the coaching staff, starting with Quizz, DJ, and Coach Wilson. After a slow start, we picked up some momentum when Offensive Coordinator Pat Matthews produced all of the game videos. I appreciate the patience from everybody as we recreated that magical season.

I have to thank my wife, Joy, who got the unenviable task of reading the early versions of the manuscript when it simply was not very good. It was a dose of reality that I needed. After many rewrites, I was able to produce something that began to resemble a story.

I want to thank my copyeditor Book Echoes Media, for whipping everything into shape. I'm certain looking at the work of a first-time author is no easy task. Many thanks to Steve for all of the technical help with the interior and the awesome cover design (KUHN Design Group). It takes so much to get a book from all those floating ideas in one's head to the bookstore shelf.

I appreciate John P Lopez, the "OG", from Sports Radio 610 and a fellow Aggie, for doing the Foreword. And, also to the General, John McClain, from the Houston Chronicle for his kind words. I wanted this book to be something all sports enthusiasts would enjoy, but especially those who were actually close to the story.

Lastly, a special shout out to the family and friends of the team, especially Ms. Tee and Uncle Rodney, for their special insights. My hope in capturing this story was to keep it in our memories forever, and bring a smile to the faces of those who were there and knew it all so well. It was a fun time to be associated with Lamar Consolidated and those Mighty Mustangs.